# LIVING
*By*
## CHANCE
*Or By*
# CHOICE

## Books by Neva Coyle

Abiding Study Guide
Daily Thoughts on Living Free
Diligence Study Guide
Discipline Study Guide
Discipline tape album (4 cassettes) with guide
Free to Be Thin, The All-New (with Marie Chapian)
Free to Be Thin Lifestyle Plan, The All-New
Free to Be Thin Cookbook
Free to Be Thin Daily Planner
Free to Dream
Freedom Study Guide
Learning to Know God
Living By Chance or By Choice
Living Free
Living Free Seminar Study Guide
Making Sense of Pain and Struggle
Meeting the Challenges of Change
A New Heart . . . A New Start
Obedience Study Guide
Overcoming the Dieting Dilemma
Perseverance Study Guide
Restoration Study Guide
Slimming Down and Growing Up (with Marie Chapian)
There's More to Being Thin Than Being Thin (with Marie Chapian)

# LIVING
## By
# CHANCE
## Or By
# CHOICE

### How to
Respond to Circumstances
and Make Decisions With
Courage and Clear Thinking

# NEVA COYLE AND
# ZANE ANDERSON

# BETHANY HOUSE PUBLISHERS
MINNEAPOLIS, MINNESOTA 55438

Published by Bethany House Publishers
A Ministry of Bethany Fellowship, Inc.
11300 Hampshire Avenue South
Minneapolis, Minnesota 55438

Printed in the United States of America.

**Library of Congress Cataloging-in-Publication Data**

Coyle, Neva, 1943–
    Living by chance or by choice / Neva Coyle, Zane Anderson
       p.  cm.

    1. Decision-making—Religious aspects—Christianity.
I. Anderson, Zane.  II. Title.
BV4509.5.C68    1994
248.4—dc20                               94–38360
ISBN 1–55661–486–1                       CIP

I'd like to dedication this book with generous appreciation

To Neva Coyle:
Who believed enough in God's gift in me
to come alongside and challenge me
to open my thoughts and heart and put them into print.

To Leroy Cloud:
My pastor and my father in the faith,
the one whose wisdom and commitment helped me
at many significant crossroads in my life.

To the flock that I now pastor:
What a wonderful body of believers.
Their patience, their love, and their commitment
has helped me become whom God has
called me to be.

To my children:
Don't forget. Make the wise choices
and enjoy His destiny for your lives.

Most importantly to my bride:
My wife, the woman who has so powerfully
impacted my life.
Next to Christ, she was the wisest choice I ever made,
and I am so glad she agreed with my choice.
I love you, Jan.

Zane Anderson

NEVA COYLE is Founder of Overeaters Victorious and President of Neva Coyle Ministries. Her ministry is enhanced by her bestselling books and tapes, as well as by her being a gifted motivational speaker/teacher. Neva and her husband make their home in California.

ZANE ANDERSON is the Senior Pastor of Mountain Christian Center in Oakhurst, California. He is a graduate of Bethany Bible College and has a strong ministry at youth camps, college conferences, singles retreats, churches, as well as ministries overseas. Under his leadership, Mountain Christian Center has grown into a vibrant church, offering both a K–12 Christian school and preschool.

## ACKNOWLEDGMENTS

Special thanks to Kris Rich who tediously transcribed end-less hours of Zane's many messages on Crossroads and Choices. Also to Pastor Roy Worley, Sheri Grimes, and Nancy Carroll who listened with untold patience to Neva as she pounded out the concepts and experimented with analogies and illustrations. And, of course, our editor David Hazard who helped us through the rough places and the challenging cross-roads all authors face when working to bring cohesiveness and order to abstract thought. God bless you.

# Contents

PART THREE:
Successful Crossroads Navigators Learn to
Become People of Purpose

PART FOUR:
Successful Crossroads Navigators Live Principled Lives

# 1

# Life at the Crossroads

"Get the camera. We've got to have a picture of this!" What parent hasn't marked the significant events of their child's life and development with snapshots? A first birthday, the first day of school . . . graduation from college. We want to capture forever the exact moment when someone we love makes the transition from one phase of life to another. Things will never be the same.

There are other moments of change, however, that are not recorded with snapshots. Other times when a change challenges our sense of security, or leaves us struggling to find the right new direction. We may think, *I wish someone would give me a clear picture of what I should do. Or a clear map that would tell me the right road to choose now. I need direction . . . and I need to know how to make wise choices.*

For some of you, this "crossroads" came up abruptly and unexpectedly. Perhaps you have lost a job, or someone who was close to you. You're faced with choices you never planned for, and don't even want to make. Circumstances are forcing you out of where you have been settled and comfortable . . . and now what?

What makes it worse is that the road behind you is closed

and barricaded. You can't go back, but you are unsure how to go on. Fear and dread are suddenly constant companions, and you know that you have to overcome these overwhelming emotions in order to make the best decisions. But your emotions have become like misbehaving kids in the passenger side of the car—they keep jumping around, even blocking your view of the road ahead, taking all your attention from the task of safely steering. Fear itself—the fear that unwanted change brings—is something you have to face even before you can make wise choices—but how do you get this dominating emotion to sit still and be quiet?

Then there are others of you who *want* change. You have grown in some way beyond the circumstances you're in. This would include the man or woman who has learned far more than their present job requires—but your vision, skills, and leadership abilities will never be used in the place where you are. You can grumble and complain that management has no vision, or you can take matters into your own hands and head for a new place where your talents will be used to your satisfaction. This would also include people who find that what they want from life, from a church, from a community, has simply changed—and again, the need is to "pack up the boxes" and scout out new territory.

So many Christians also become sidetracked, talking themselves *out* of change. Sometimes they are genuinely confused by certain false views of the Christian life. "Christians shouldn't have any ambitions or dreams. They just get in the way of God's will," one young friend was told. This assumes that God cannot plant a dream or a hope in someone's heart. This kind of thinking hampers a number of Christians, keeping them from taking the risks necessary for growth and change—and often from fulfilling God's true purpose for being here in this life.

We want to say, categorically, that God *does* give vision, ambition, and desire for change. Sometimes it begins as a restlessness and not always with clear direction attached. For some time you may feel your "inner compass" being pulled by a different pole, pointing you in a new or different direction. Then you know your life is at a crossroads. You need to make a decision. Now what?

Or maybe you are coming to the close of one phase of your life—say, completing high school, college, or another type of training. And now "the ball is in your court." You have to make some choices.

And over and above these practical circumstances there is the fact that you know God is the only one who sees the big picture. In fact, you really want Him to give direction to your life. But *how* do we hear God? Does He only speak to us, specifically, and through prayer, saying things like, "About that job you're thinking of. Here's what you should do...." Or does He merely arrange the circumstances so that "doors of opportunity" open and others close? Do you "wait on God," or "move out in boldness"? Or maybe you think God is only concerned about the spiritual decisions, and isn't interested in directing you if you're trying to decide about a "secular job" or a "non-Christian college." As if life fell into sacred and secular categories, which, if you are a Christian, it does not.

Our position is that God cares about *all* of life, and in specific all of *your* life. And we believe that He wants to do more than direct you in any specific decisions you may need to make right now as you face your personal crossroads. (And He *does* want to help you in that decision!) But He also wants to do something more wonderful than that. He wants to help you grow from within, in spirit and in confidence, so that you go through this time of change—and all the others that life will bring to you—with a clear sense of direction in *all* that God plans for you . . . both the outer directions you should choose and the inner growth He wants to accomplish as He oversees your way through this sometimes trackless wilderness called *life.* The choices we make are important to God; but the person we become through life's changes is also important. In fact, we believe it is the key, the real beginning point.

## Making a Choice About Choices

Before we begin, it's important to help you take a look at how you approach change and making decisions. Understanding how you react when you find yourself in a crossroads moment can help you get a handle on some important issues you must address as you begin.

One way that people face decisions is to take the "muddle through" approach. If you have purchased a book to help you make right choices, the chances are good that you're not interested in doing it this way. Taking the attitude that "life will just happen to me, it's bigger than me anyway" is not the an-swer. The decision to put off taking an active role in your de-cisions *is* a decision, but not the best one. God wants us to take an active part in seeking the path and plan He has for our lives—the plan that will bring us the greatest satisfaction *and* the most glory to Him!

Another approach is to be dragged into a decision, all the while being choked with a rope of fear. Does the thought of change heap mounds of anxiety and pressure on you? Change can bring anxiety for most of us, even when it's wanted. But fear and other negative emotions cannot be swept aside, and as Christians we don't need to be ashamed of feeling afraid "because it shows you don't have enough faith." It's more helpful to learn to face your fear, understanding what you're really afraid of, and make growth steps *through* to a new level of courage and character. (If fear and anxiety are a problem for you, we want to help you, and there is a whole section in this book that will help you to grow in peace and confidence.)

Still another approach is to focus on past regrets, because of choices we made long ago that didn't "pan out" the way we'd hoped. There is a measure of fear in this approach to change, too. But *hope* is probably the operative word here. Maybe you don't dare to hope that God can redeem a real or so-called "bad decision" today, now, in the present. To live by regret is to allow our life today—and worse, *tomorrow*—to re-main chained to the past. We have a God who frees and re-deems and transforms. He is *for* you, and definitely *all for* giv-ing you a great future. You know you don't want to end up like "Uncle Harry," saying twenty years from now, "I wish I had. I could have. But I didn't. . . ."

And so we come down to choices. This book is all about the process of being changed ourselves as we learn how to make wise choices. What we hope to do is to guide you through a personal kind of "inventory" that is far different than handing you a set of absolutes, or a one-size-fits-all ap-proach. This is participatory reading, and as you enter into the process we will walk you through, we believe that a greater thing will take place, over and above the specific decision that may be pressing you right now. You will not need to be thrown by even the unplanned and unwanted. You will actually begin to get a clear sense of your path from today *toward* tomorrow, so that you understand the deeper purposes God has for you.

And when opposition, resistance, or future changes are tossed at you, you will find a new steadiness, as if a new invisible "rudder" was directing you through the gale. You will become a successful crossroads navigator, understanding how to make godly choices. You will move from being a person who is blown by the winds, to becoming a person who knows how to "tack into the wind," gaining power and momentum.

Life's crossroads—and the "crosswinds" they bring—can give us unique opportunities to see the hand of God as He orchestrates circumstances and gives us chances for personal growth. Often, times of upheaval can reveal our flaws, weaknesses, and imperfections. Most of us are alert enough to know that, in order to make new choices, certain inner changes have to take place first. What we need is to be *enlarged,* to have new living skills added to us in order to make our lives over anew. It's natural for us, as humans, to want God's comfort, when what we really need is to learn how He wants to change *us* through our circumstances. Crossroads offer the opportunity to learn to depend on God more, to love Him at a deeper level and to trust Him more than ever before. And through change He will bring us to a new place of security and peace in Him as He works out His purpose in our lives.

## Where Do I *Grow* From Here?

If you are standing at a crossroads—a place of decision—you may be wondering if you can really trust God. And shouldn't you just be making practical choices first? You may be thinking of plenty of ways you can get on with your life, quickly and without "divine" assistance.

We can assure you, nothing will satisfy you as much as knowing that you have *first* placed your life in God's hands, allowing Him to deepen your sense of purpose.

What we want to offer you is much more than a ready-reference for getting through times of change. There is a way to discover both a safe passage through the crossroads experiences and also to come out spiritually stronger and deeper. It all depends on learning certain skills, the way a ship's navigator or wilderness explorer learns how to find his way in trackless seas or forests. Through our years in both church and national ministries, we have learned solid principles to follow and eternal promises to hang your life and hope on that will help you form a map through life's changes *and* make you a stronger person on the inside.

We have observed countless people at life's various cross-roads. Certain choices you can make will give you an advantage in getting through change or upheaval. We want to pass along these guiding principles to you.

Just before we begin, there are a few questions you need to consider.

Is the very idea of change a threat to you? Is the prospect of change the same as certain disaster? Does becoming a different person seem like impending doom? Do you always see your crossroads as a crisis or a new start?

Take a little time to think about your answer before you proceed. It is urgent. Because no book can change you. Ultimately, change and growth will involve an interaction between you and God. We can pass along wise principles, and this book can be a tool in God's hands.

But *willingness* and *trust* together make the first step. Are you willing to let go of the life that used to be and trust God in new ways, at a deeper level than ever before?

*Do it!* Do trust Him!

Take a few moments, before you begin the next chapter, to pray. Trust your next step to Him—and commit to Him the whole journey, wherever change may lead you.

We promise that, once you have made this first important step you will have a new sense of God's presence with you, giving you courage in place of fear. Quiet calm in place of restlessness or anxiety.

The journey you are on, if you choose to go—is about to become very exciting!

# *Part One*

## Secrets of Successful Crossroads Navigators

# 2

# Life in the Crash Position

---

### Secret #1

### Know the difference between a cross-roads and a crisis.

---

Can you identify with any of the following statements?

☐ One minute everything was great—and the next it felt as if my whole world was turned upside down.

☐ I thought I was as secure as the next person—but I tell you, I can't bear the thought of making the moves I need to make.

☐ You could knock me over with a feather—I never dreamed it would be this hard to make a decision and stick with it. I've always hated indecision.

☐ I'm completely wiped out by what's happened to me. And I'm overwhelmed by the choices I have to make.

☐ My faith feels as though it's below rock-bottom, and just when I need it the most.

What do you do when you feel so overwhelmed you can't begin to make the choices you need to make?

When faced with some of the most important decisions and choices, something seems to get in the way. Change—and the fear that comes with it. Whether or not you have seen yourself to be a decisive person in other regards, major crossroads can find you paralyzed. Impending change threatens as loud as impending doom. *Choices! Decisions! Change! Crisis!*

The brave man or woman inside you suddenly wants to assume the crash position. On top of paralysis comes a sense of shame, and a voice inside begins to dump on you, telling what a coward you are. *This is a voice you need to silence at once!*

## Crossroads or Crisis?

The best way to move beyond fear is to check your own attitude toward your circumstances. A crossroads is not always a crisis—even though crisis usually presents a crossroads.

Thankfully, in real life, we rarely have to assume the crash position.

Just as it would be hard to breathe while doubled-over holding your ankles, it is pretty impossible to maintain optimism and faith in that emotional position. Hard to envision a turnaround with your head tucked between your knees. Maybe the change you're facing represents risk and failure. No wonder, then, you have been wasting effort by avoiding crucial choices. But change doesn't always have to represent a fatal nose dive and certain catastrophe. And it's up to you—*you* must make the choice to stop *avoiding*. To face your life again—do it now!

*1. Change your position—change your perspective.* Important and wonderful things can happen at life's crossroads—if we'll just let our emotions relax from the crash position.

For just a moment, why not back off and take an objective look at your circumstances—one that's free of emotions. Can you be objective long enough to see the possibilities instead of the impossibilities overwhelming you at the moment? If you can do so, you may be able to experience the beginning of a brand new season of God's purpose and power.

What lies in the pages that follow is more than just an opportunity to make changes, but a step-by-step guide to help you. If you are willing to open up your perspective, you can see changes in priorities, refocused vision, renewed commitments, and brand new goals—all as a result of your crossroads experience. And as you follow these steps you will not only see changes in your present circumstances, you will develop new living skills that add up to a new *you*!

*2. Your impossibilities can become possibilities.* Are there dreams you would like to reclaim? Goals you want to redefine? Do you need hope to be reborn? Do you want to get on track with God's plans? Crossroads experiences bring us to the threshold of those wonderful changes. Things you thought impossible can become goals and certainties.

*3. Choose to let Jesus be involved.* This can be a new season of God's grace for you. Jesus can bind up even your deepest, most private wounds. Even if you are bound by past experiences and failure, He is the Liberator. Living a life filled with the favor of the Lord is promised to you. He wants to be your Champion, Defender, and Comforter. The dead ashes scattered about in your life can be exchanged for beauty. Praise can replace your despair. You can experience glorious confidence instead of continuing to live in fear and dread of change and choice. (See Isaiah 61:1–3.)

No doubt about it, a crossroads requires decisions. Furthermore, these decisions aren't just limited to options such as what shall I do? and where shall I go? They're the stepping-stones to what you can *be*—open doors to what you can *become*. The choice is yours—to change and to be changed.

## Relaxing

Have you put yourself in the crash position emotionally? Fear of impending disaster can be replaced with new joy and confidence as you rediscover the hand of God moving in your life. Can you take the chance? Will you let go of fear and step out in a new vision of life filled with security and confidence in God? If so, you will begin to learn the rich lessons of the crossroads experience. Choose to trust God, and you will learn the important principles of living a life that is free and empowered.

There is a vast difference between a crossroads and a crisis—and the ones who can tell the difference are those who decide to approach change in a *praise position*. This is more than a secret, it's a choice—a choice you will have to make.

What is your decision?

# 3

# Why Pray?

---

### Secret #2

### You can do more than pray—you can
### know *why* you are praying!

---

"Honest to God"—Hank raised his right hand for emphasis—"I had no idea it would be this hard on the kids when Sarah went back to work. They're not happy being left with the babysitter, and Sarah feels guilty for leaving them. Our kids are top priority. But if my wife doesn't work, we'll never be able to save enough money to buy a house. We just don't know what to do."

Margie sat on the couch wringing her hands. "My husband and I are so scared. Our son is tearing the entire household apart with his abusiveness and arguing. We were hoping he'd get over it—you know, a phase he would soon be through. What can we do? Now we have to make some hard choices. But what if we do the wrong thing and push him out of our lives—or drive him away from the Lord forever?"

Maybe you can identify with Hank or with Margie. If you're

like most people, you have probably come to the point at some time where you felt forced to make a choice—all the while shaking your head and wondering where you would get that extra nudge that indicates which option would be the best. Pretty soon you are really up against a wall, feeling the pressure. What makes this so bad is that you know decisions made under pressure can be less than the best—and you still have to live with them! Why is it the experience you've gained making other choices hasn't prepared you for making the choice you face today?

So where do we go for answers and help in making our decisions?

The place to begin is in prayer—maybe at a new level of prayer and trust than you have experienced before. Prayer is the first skill you need in walking safely through your crossroads decision.

Unfortunately, it's often the last thing people turn to—as if God were "the last resort."

## Is God in Charge?

One day several dedicated Christians were asked: "Is God always in charge?" "Of course," each one responded. One went on to add—"Yes, He is in charge, once you allow Him to be. Why do you ask?"

"Just this," said the interviewer. "If God is in charge—if He is truly in control, why pray?"

It's a valid question that every seeking believer comes to grips with at one time or another. Especially in light of verses like Acts 15:18, which indicate that the Lord has known how things will turn out from the beginning (See Acts 15:19), or Romans 8, which many interpret as saying, "God will work everything out for good—so relax and let it happen."

If someone asked you the question *Why pray?*, what would you say?

Most of us realize that there is no such thing as accepting Christ, then placing everything in God's hands and putting our lives on autopilot. The Christian life is not just sitting back to passively receive His blessings and experience His love—like a packaged vacation tour. Living under His sovereignty is not a once-and-for-all putting Him in charge. It is learning to relate to Him every day in new and deeper ways.

## Partnership With God

The Christian life is lived in partnership with God. It is being linked to His power, rooted in His strength and wisdom. Prayer is where that transaction occurs. It is where His life is poured into us. In the very moment we bow before His *lordship* we are exposed to His *majesty*. When we submit, we are lifted up. In prayerful worship we find the security we need to completely open ourselves to His love. It is where we discover how to escape the tyranny of the flesh and fight victoriously over temptation. Prayer is where we find answers, direction, and perspective. It is where God reveals His heart—the purposes and the plans He has outlined for our lives.

Knowing all this doesn't make it any easier to find or make the time to pray. The question we need to ask, then, is *Why don't we pray?*

## Maybe We Don't Pray Because . . .

Under the pressure of daily responsibilities, many of us fail to pray and seek God regularly. It's not that we're unconcerned with God's opinion or don't want His direction, but in the busy-ness of life we simply neglect prayer. How many of us have not experienced the feeling of coming into a church service thinking, "I haven't prayed in some time. . . ." The very thing we should not neglect—our prayer life—is often the first thing we do neglect. Most especially, when we are under pressure.

Other reasons for failing to pray may have a deeper cause. Sometimes prayer means having to face and deal with a problem once we admit it to God. We may also have to face our lack of faith. Or perhaps, under the stress, we simply are not willing to do the hard work of trusting. Some of us, facing decisions, simply "move to a new address"—find a way to avoid facing and resolving the conflicts that have come to the surface.

## The Do-It-Yourself Christian

Some of us, avoiding prayer, *pump* instead. We lift weights, so to speak, by carrying burdens we were never intended to carry. We may pride ourselves on being survivors—

claiming each experience makes us stronger, wiser, and more able to cope on our own without the crutch of prayer and the dependence it fosters. Secretly, we may be harboring the attitude that prayer is too passive—that when it comes right down to it, God wants us to pick ourselves up and get to work. Wrong. How very wrong we are.

## The Deadly Trap of Indifference

Another reason some of us avoid prayer is simply indifference. Sometimes we just grow cold and don't care about God's presence and power. Coming to a crossroads, we simply close our eyes, lean back, and hope for the best.

But most of us realize that neglect, avoidance, and indifference don't work. We want to be more involved with God and understand His plans. We have discovered that to know Him means we must become people of prayer.

## We Pray Because . . .

. . . we want to focus in on God. We long to know who He is, and what He is doing. We pray because it is the way we discover how He works, and it serves as a wonderful way to remind ourselves repeatedly why we have put Him in charge. We read: "Look to the Lord and His strength; seek His face always. Remember the wonders He has done . . ."[1] and we know that can only happen when we pray.

. . . we want to ask that His purpose and will be done. We don't want to live with a "whatever will be, will be" philosophy. But like Jesus we need the opportunity to say, "Nevertheless, Your will be done . . ."[2]

. . we have a desire to tap into His power. We want to realize the truth of "remain in me and my words remain in you" asking whatever we wish and seeing it happen[3] and believing we will receive whatever we ask for in prayer.[4]

. . . we choose prayer to be our first resource, not our last resort. It is because we elect to pray that we are able to distin-

[1] 1 Chronicles 16:11–13
[2] Luke 22:42 KJV
[3] John 15:7
[4] Matthew 21:22

guish the essentials from the non-essentials when we make our decisions. Prayer helps us sift our possessions, examine the issues, and explore ideas. Prayer is where we give birth to our dreams and find the courage to set goals. It is where we store up for ourselves treasures in heaven.[5]

. . . we have an unquenched thirst for a deeper relationship with God—"They will call on my name and I will answer them; I will say, 'They are my people,' and they will say, 'The Lord is our God.' "[6]

. . . we know prayer is what puts our fleshly appetites and motives on notice. It's where we learn to set our minds on the things of the Spirit and take them off the things of the flesh.[7] Prayer is the soil where the roots of self are uprooted and the seedlings of the fruit of the Holy Spirit are planted, cultivated, and fed.[8]

. . . we know it robs the devil of the opportunity to get a toehold into the matters of our lives and a grip on our hearts.[9] In prayer, we open to the Lord all our emotional pain and sad memories and the family roots that want to spring forth like so many weeds in our lives. In opening to the Lord we take territory away from the enemy of our souls. When in prayer we lay down our anger, unforgiveness, and bitterness—we destroy the adversary's hold on our attitudes and actions.

## A Prayer-Way of Life

Yes, of course we pray, not merely because of habit, and certainly not because of a form or ritual we go through. We pray because God means for it to become our way of life. We pray *with* purpose and we pray *on* purpose. We pray *with* and *for* power. We pray often and with a sense of mission.

Throughout the time you are reading this book, set aside specific time to pray. Be open to God, listening to what He wants to show you about yourself and your life's direction. Decide to be free about telling Him your dreams, disappointments—whatever is on your heart.

And remember, His voice is still the most important voice

---

[5]Matthew 6:20
Zechariah 13:9
[7]Romans 8:5
[8]Galatians 5:19–23
[9]Ephesians 4:27

in your prayer dialogue. Be open to His comfort *and* correction, direction to move *and* the signal to wait.

Remember, always, He is the Lord of Life. And in particular, the Lord of *your* life. Freely give Him that place.

# 4

# When You Pray

---

### Secret #3

### Let God show you *how* to pray.

---

Janet sank deeper into her chair and took in a long breath. "I just don't know what to do. I have to make a decision soon. Time is running out."

"Have you prayed about this?" the counselor asked.

"I know I should, but . . . well, that's why I've come to see you. I thought you might be able to help me sort this all out."

As it turned out, Janet knew she *should* pray—but she was so overwhelmed by the pressure to make a decision and boggled by the options, she just didn't know *how* to pray. All she needed was someone to get her going in the right direction.

The majority of Christians agree that "there is a personal God who watches over us, and can be reached through our prayers."[1] But believing that God answers our prayers is not

---

[1]"Born Again: A Look at Christians in America," A Barna Report, Barna Research Group, Glendale, California, 1990.

enough if we don't pray. F. B. Meyer said, "The great tragedy of life is not unanswered prayer, but in unoffered prayer."

In times of decision-making, we can't afford *unoffered* prayers.

"When you pray," Jesus says, "go into your room, close the door and pray to your Father. . . ."[2] When—not if. If we are to ever find our way safely through the crossroads experiences and make the right decisions, we need to take the first all-important step of prayer. How do we begin? Here are some basic steps that will help you start.

*1. Be open and vulnerable as you talk to the Lord.* No matter how much confusion or pressure you are facing you can enter the place of prayer with our Father assured of complete safety. In His presence, you can let down all your defenses with no fear of being misused or rejected.

Don't be afraid to be honest. Be as open as you can, pouring out your needs and requests. Rosalind Rinker says, "Prayer is the expression of the human heart in conversation with God. The more natural the prayer, the more real He becomes. It has all been simplified for me to this extent: prayer is a dialogue between two people who love each other."[3]

*2. Expect things to begin to change.* When you pray—from an undecorated, unpretentious heart—He promises to meet you. "You will seek me and find me when you seek me with *all* your heart."[4]

When we choose to be vulnerable before Him, we can expect His response and answer. The psalmist said, "In the morning, O LORD, you hear my voice; in the morning I lay my requests before you and wait in expectation."[5]

It is not only God's presence and answer that we can expect—we can also expect circumstances to begin to change. Once God starts moving, things cannot remain the same.

If you have ever viewed the damage following an earthquake, you will see a new depth of meaning in the words from Hebrews: ". . . the removing of what can be shaken . . . so that what cannot be shaken may remain" (12:27).

The truth is, once God begins to move in response to our prayers, it can sometimes seem as though our whole world is

---

[2]Matthew 6:6
[3]*Prayer: Conversing With God*, Rosalind Rinker, Zondervan Books, 1959.
[4]Jeremiah 29:13 (italics added)
[5]Psalm 5:3

shaking beyond control. Some of our preconceived ideas of how God should or should not answer may need to be shaken. At first, things may seem to be getting worse, not better. If God is our safety, how can this be?

Sometimes the things we ask require a change in us before our prayers can be answered. "O Lord, give me a wonderful wife," is a prayer some Christian men offer—and that may result in God working to change the pray-er into a husband suitable for such a terrific woman. "I want a husband who sees a wife as a full partner," some women pray—and that may mean that God needs to do a work of cooperation deep within. He begins to topple points of control, expose manipulative tendencies, and enlarge a willingness to shoulder responsibility.

Sometimes before God can give us the answers to our prayers, He must weaken the foundations of power we have built by ourselves. We ask for freedom, God points out our habits. We pray for liberty, God exposes our bondages. We pray for a ministry, God reveals our lack of servanthood and submission.

*3. Expect God to speak* into *your life.* When we open ourselves to God through prayer, we can expect Him to speak clearly. When God spoke the light into existence, He spoke *into* darkness and created the light. And the light He spoke forth invaded the darkness and has done so ever since.

When God speaks *into* your darkness you can expect Him to create a new light of understanding to invade the confusion and fear. Just as He separated the light from the darkness, He can separate and clarify the issues and options you face today.

*4. Pray in Jesus' name.* "And I will do whatever you ask in my name, so that the Son may bring glory to the Father. You may ask me for anything in my name, and I will do it."[6] Can you believe such a promise? We who have been given the right—the authority to use His name—*the name above all names*—can we ever know how much power and privilege this promise gives us with God?

We have every reason to need this kind of access to God. One can barely imagine dropping a business card at the gates of heaven and receiving any recognition at all. But when in prayer we approach the portals of heaven, just mentioning the name of Jesus opens not only the outer gates but ushers us into

---

[6]John 14:13–14

the private quarters of our Father God. No appointment necessary. Walk-ins welcome. When we use the right name—the name of Jesus.

*5. Pray* power *prayers.* Power prayers are not necessarily loud or commanding. Power prayers come from an attitude of the heart.

Power prayers are those offered in childlike trust, from the place of need. The prayer that comes from the heart in sweet relationship with God, as a child before his "papa." The honest prayer is the one in which all needs and desires are simply put before Him.

Power prayers come from a heart that has confidence in God. So confident of His care that we can lay our confusing options before Him, expecting Him to help us make the right decisions.

*6. Admit you can't do this on your own.* It is a mysterious fact that God requires our prayers. He answers only the *prayed* prayer, fills only the *admitted* need, and sends reinforcement only to the *powerless.* Why? This story illustrates the answer:

A man with a deformed hand stood in church during a service. There was a guest speaker that night and it was expected that he'd be a little different than what the congregation was used to. The man stood back, wanting to hear, but not really wanting to be seen. He had become used to keeping his hand hidden, tucked inside his coat—and himself tucked away in the corner. The speaker, however, lived up to his reputation of boldness and pointed to the man.

"Come here," he said. "Stand up here in front of everyone."

The congregation was silent. They knew about the deformity and the man's reticence. They waited in expectation.

"Stretch out your hand," said the preacher.

The man might have said, "Why do I have to do that?" But instead, he realized he was at a crossroads—he could choose to risk and reach, or protect and keep his limitation.

Slowly, he pulled his hand from inside the coat . . . and felt the fingers and joints miraculously unlock. . . .

You probably recognize the story.[7] Are you willing to expose to Jesus your need? He invites us to lay it out before Him—and so often we say, "He knows what I need. I'll just

---

[7]Mark 3:3–5

wait here, and let Him get around to me, but I won't expose my need."

What would have happened if the man had not taken his hand out of his coat and stretched it toward Jesus? He would have preserved some dignity—but never gotten his answer. This is what happens to us when we refuse to "stretch forth" our need.

You see, exposing our need is the way we admit we can't provide the best answer on our own.

"What do you want?" Jesus asked some blind men.[8] Silly question for Jesus, wouldn't you say? "We want to receive our sight—we want to see. We don't want to be blind anymore." They simply admitted their need and their powerlessness to make it happen.

The Lord's response was one of *compassion*. The Bible says He touched them. Won't you let His compassion be directed toward you and touch you, as well?

*7. Let no thought or aspect of your heart remain hidden from Him.* It is one thing to be vulnerable and transparent, another to trust Him enough to admit your need. It is quite another to open the heart so wide that it's not just our prayers that are exposed to Him, but our true *selves*.

And that is what the crossroads of life are all about: growing in our *selves*, as we are taught and led and changed by God our Father.

It can be a daring new discovery, this deepening prayer experience. It can also be threatening. Some of us have been betrayed by unthinking people who did not know how to be confidential, and we have difficulty trusting even God. Now is the time to expose the scars inflicted by one of "God's children," so that we no longer recoil when God himself wants to touch us.

If you want to safely take the right steps through the crossroads you now face, you can discover a new dimension to prayer. This *is* the time—no doubt about it—the time for you to make still another choice.

*Will you trust God—more fully than ever before?*

Take time right now—and pray. Ask God to help you remove all barriers and limitations that you may have set up to protect yourself. You will begin to feel free again.

---

[8]Matthew 20:30–34

# 5

# Prayer Is Relationship

---

### Secret #4

**Rediscover the truth that prayer is more
about relationship than about requests.**

---

Confident that Grandpa will not consider him an intrusion,
the little boy enters his grandfather's room and approaches his
chair. Holding out a box he says, "Can you help me, Papa?"

Grandpa lays down his paper and opens his arms to this
cherished child. "What do we have here?"

"It's my puzzle," the boy says, "but it's too hard for me."

They sit at a nearby table and dump the colorful pieces in
a big pile in the center. Grandpa rubs his chin. "First, let's turn
them all right-side-up, and set the cover where we can see it.
It's easier to make a puzzle if we can see the picture we're suppose to be making."

The boy reaches for one piece. Then another. "Look, I think
these go together," he says.

"Now don't be too hasty," says Grandpa. . . .

"See . . . I can *make* them fit."

After nearly ruining these pieces—and several others—the boy almost gives up in frustration. "I don't like this. It's too hard. Let's quit."

"Now hold on," says Grandpa patiently. "If we start to work from this corner piece, we can get going the right way."

For a few moments, the boy leans against his grandfather, watching him carefully fit the pieces together.

Suddenly he snatches a piece of the puzzle from Grandpa's hand. "Not this one, I don't like this one."

"What's wrong with it?" the old man smiles.

"I don't like this color. It's too dark. See?" He holds it up for inspection. "I like this *other* one better," he says as he reaches for a bright piece with flowers on it.

"But the dark pieces are important too. We'll need them."

"But I don't like them," he pouts.

For a moment, Grandpa watches as the boy separates the pieces—bright and desirable colors in one area, dark and undesirable in another.

"There, let's make the picture from these pieces. They're my favorites," he says at last.

"It won't work, little one," Grandpa says lovingly. "To get the picture, you need all the pieces—not just the pretty ones. Look." He reaches for the box lid, with the picture on it. "This is what it's supposed to look like."

"But I don't like the ugly pieces," the boy says.

"They're only ugly when they're not put together. Once it's all finished you won't even see them. You'll just see the beautiful picture."

Many of us know how frustrating it is to be unable to finish a jigsaw puzzle because of a missing piece or two. Yet, we can be much like this child when we come to God with the pieces of our lives all scattered about us. We ask for wisdom—but resist the experiences that will cultivate wisdom within us. Reaching for the pretty pieces, we say to God, "I only like the nice colors. Could you put the pieces of my life together *without* dark colors?"

We ask for guidance, but instead of looking at God's view of what our life is to be, we pick and choose, sort and separate. We pray for direction, but resist when it's given. We can even tell God, "I love you"—then go away from prayer looking for something more enjoyable to do. Let Him finish our puzzle, we say. We may even tell ourselves we have left the problem with Him—and that sounds good. It is true that God holds all the pieces of our puzzled situations in His hand—but He needs our active cooperation, our partnership, to put the whole picture together.

God wants us *present* and *involved* when He is guiding our lives. He could put all the pieces together, of course. He could even do it easier and quicker alone. But the point is for us to work on it together. It is working together *in and on* a project that causes people to know each other better. And in the case of our growth and guidance, we have a choice to make: We can choose to make the *answer* to our circumstances the priority, or we can put our *relationship* with the Lord first.

God's first priority is not the ministry, but the minister. The mission is never more important than the missionary. The messenger always comes before the message. You see, Jesus stands before the Father interceding on our behalf. It is not our work He presents first to God—but us.

No question, this *is* the big dividing point: We must choose the kind of relationship we want with God. Either it will be one in which we choose our own way and ask God to bless it—or we surrender to Him, giving ourselves into His hands to be re-made as He chooses.

## Why Do We Struggle?

We get discouraged, don't we? The pieces of our lives and the options available to us lying on the table makes no sense and show very little promise of becoming a complete picture. We become confused and even bored. Wanting a quick solution, we try to fit pieces together that weren't even designed to fit except as they are joined with other pieces. We want action and answers, not help. We ask God to do it—to put the pieces together, when He wants to trust us with the pieces one by one and show us where they fit.

*But, that's so slow!* When we pray, staying in God's presence, in partnership with Him, it is true that we may not be able to see results immediately. The answers to our prayers and the effects of our prayers may not be discernable right away. But having the answer to our prayers is not where our rest and strength comes from—it is found only in Him.

Find rest, O my soul, in God alone; my hope comes

from Him. He alone is my rock and my salvation; He is my fortress, I will not be shaken. My salvation and my honor depend on God; He is my mighty rock, my refuge. Trust in Him at all times, O people; pour out your hearts to Him, for God is our refuge.[1]

It may even seem as though God is not working. But our trust is not based on what we *see* Him doing, our trust is based on *knowing* Him. We are learning to live by faith, not by sight.[2]

In the waiting, we cultivate obedience and faithfulness. It's the time we can best learn to experience deep intimacy with God.

"Be joyful in hope, patient in affliction, faithful in prayer."[3]

When we are this close to God, it's because we choose to be this close to Him. When we elect to bring the pieces—the options we face, the choices we must consider—we are also choosing a deep intimacy with our Father, not just a quick fix or simple solution. And when we do, it's no wonder we often encounter what seems to be a reversal or point of struggle. Even opposition. We may pick up a piece or two—even in the intimacy of God's presence—and try to force them to fit together in a way *we* want them to fit. Right there, knowing that God is watching, our fleshly desires and self-motivations can surface.

Besides the struggles with our own lower nature, we must never forget that we have an adversary—an enemy—that would try unceasingly to discourage or distract us from being this close to God. If you feel guilt or shame for leaving God's presence and expecting Him to work out all your problems, you can be sure it does not come from Him.

God invites us to return, to begin anew. It is God who wants us to have another go at it. It is our Father who waits with the puzzle pieces safely in His care until we return. He could finish the picture without us—and certainly without our interference. Let's be honest, though. If He fixed all the messes we bring to Him, we would learn to dump them in His lap and walk away. Our relationship with Him would be reduced to

---

[1]Psalm 62:5–8
[2]2 Corinthians 5:7
[3]Romans 12:12

the unimportance of an errand—the way we drop our clothes by the dry cleaners.

The Bible says Jesus told his disciples they should always pray and not give up.[4] It says we should pray continually,[5] that we can enter God's private quarters any time.

As a child, I (Neva) was excited when my mother sent my sisters and me to the store. It was quite a walk. Mom gave us a list, tucked it in an envelope in one of our pockets, and out the door we went. The store owner was Mom's cousin, and no matter how many customers she had in the store we were always greeted cheerfully. Even before she took the note or gathered the items together, we were welcomed behind the counter right into her apartment where she spent a little time fussing over us. Other customers stayed in the store, they didn't belong behind the counter or in her private apartment. The front area was for business, only family members were invited to go in the back.

That's the way it is with God. No matter how many times we come, we never find Him too busy with the affairs of the world, and we never catch Him off guard. Our Father is never too busy for us. He doesn't just gather up the items on our list and fill our requests and send us on our way like satisfied customers. He greets us warmly and invites us into the place He saves for family—into His personal quarters.

> Therefore, brothers, since we have confidence to enter the Most Holy Place by the blood of Jesus, by a new and living way opened for us through the curtain, that is, His body, and since we have a great priest over the house of God, let us draw near to God with a sincere heart in full assurance of faith, having our hearts sprinkled to cleanse us from a guilty conscience and having our bodies washed with pure water. Let us hold unswervingly to the hope we profess, for He who promised is faithful.[6]

Isn't it time you answered God's invitation to come into the area He reserves for "family"? Like the boy with the puzzle, bring the options and pressing decisions you are facing into God's presence. Lay them all out before Him, the light pieces and the dark. Let Him begin to hand you each piece in order,

---

[4]Luke 18:1
[5]1 Thessalonians 5:17
[6]Hebrews 10:19–23

instructing you on how to fit each piece together. You see, He knows *how* to put the pieces together, because He designed the picture. Only He can spot a piece that doesn't belong. And if a piece seems to be missing, ask Him—He is probably holding it in His possession.

In this process, you can experience something so wonderful you will not be able to find the exact words to express it. In your intimate moments with God, within the circle of His arms, you will find the pieces of your decision coming together. More than that you will find the fractured segments of your personality, your heart, your motives—your real *self* being put together as well.

The real miracle is not that persevering in prayer changes *things* but that it changes *the one who prays.* "Perseverance must finish its work," the Bible says. It's not just hanging in there until our prayers are answered, but until the perseverance itself does its work as well— ". . . that you may be mature and complete, not lacking anything."[7] Without need—needing nothing! Can you imagine? Can you dare to believe it?

You may protest: *I've been doing that. I have been hanging in there. I've been persevering in prayer. I've yielded my will and surrendered my life to God. Waiting in His presence I know what He is showing me to do—yet . . . I still seem unable to do anything about it. It seems as though I am still stuck at square one.*

Remember, we started out to find safe passage through our crossroads—to find the wisdom with which to consider the options and make right decisions.

Let's not underestimate the importance of prayer at our crossroads. But remember that it is the *first* step toward our goal. Many discover that they can stop living in *the crash position*, and that they can take this crucial first step of prayer, but they suddenly freeze as they tentatively attempt the next step. Though they experience God's grace, love, and intimacy, they run headlong into other sources of power at work in their lives. And in the decision-making process, they stop dead in their tracks.

Is it possible to be tapped into God's power, but gripped by other sources of power at the same time? Yes, it is.

Now it is time to confront the other "voices of power" in your life.

---

[7]James 1:4

# 6

# The Power Voices

---

**Secret #5**

**Learn to identify all the "voices of
power" in your life and decide to listen
only to God's voice.**

---

Let's say that your spirit is awakened to God—fully open
to Him in prayer. Your enthusiasm for God is running at full
speed, and you attempt to take another step through your
crossroads. Ready to try what you have heard the Lord whisper into your spirit, you arise one morning and say, "This is
the day. I'm going to do it!"

However, something insidious tugs at your inner self. A
doubt pushes into your mind and creeps down into your heart.
It leaves a trail of misgivings everywhere. You make a decision
all right—you decide to *wait*. Maybe tomorrow would be a better day to begin. After all, once the decision is made, life could
be forever different—another day or two isn't going to make
that much difference. . . .

What happened here? Why does it seem so impossible to carry out decisions sometimes—even decisions made in prayer? Isn't God in charge? Haven't we given Him control of our lives? What other power could possibly work against the purposes and plans of God for us?

Remember, prayer is only the *first* step in finding our way safely through the turning points of life. Though every crossroads is a definite opportunity for growth—and may even present a most positive and welcome change!—we can still freeze in our tracks, just when we want to step forward. *If that has been your experience you need the message of this crucial chapter.*

Maybe for some there is no question of stopping or going back. Maybe your circumstances just will not allow it. Your life has been forced into the change mode. And now you find yourself surrounded by a dense fog, causing you to hug the center line. You wish you were already through the intersection or back home safe and sound in bed! Anxiety builds and you wish you didn't have to make decisions. But there's no turning back. Like Peter, you finally step out of the boat and find that the water you are being invited to walk upon would be so much easier if it weren't just so . . . well, you know, *deep.*

All of us experience the trauma of *uncertainty.* Because while God's power is at work, there are other powers at work, as well.

While God is lovingly urging us forward, all the powers of an opposition are shoving you back. For all the wonderful, encouraging things the Holy Spirit breathes into our troubled minds, there are other voices clamoring to be heard. We will not get into the matter of whether these come from spiritual entities or are the voices of our own fears. Nonetheless, they are voices of power because they control what we choose to do, causing us to act or freeze.

## Emotional Dumps and Spiritual Traps

One of the voices of power you may already recognize is *the voice of the past.* Mistakes, failures, and previous disastrous decisions speak loudly and are hardly silenced without putting up a fight. *You did it once, you're bound to do it again,* says the voice of the past. *You'll never make it—just look at your track record.* Shadows from past mistakes shadow our hope for the future.

The voice of regret is another readily recognizable voice. *If I'd only been quicker, slower, spontaneous, more organized.* Regret is never satisfied. No matter how you answer it, it has a comeback of a different kind. Regret takes its lessons from another voice, the voice of expectation. *I really didn't think you'd do any better,* or *I had such high hopes for you, I'm really disappointed that you settled for "okay" when you could have been the best.*

Even the voice of past success can all but drown out the Lord's direction to try new things or to move in a different direction. *That will never work! You're stepping out of your area of experience. You'll be sorry. . . .*

Our personal history is not the only power voice we must confront. We often bring the sordid history of the entire family along as well. Digging deep into our memories we are able to pinpoint a comment that we have worn as a label ever since. "Why do you always ruin everything?" a careless parent might have said. "Why are you so slow at everything?" or "You can't do anything right!" Such comments become part of a collection of memories, preserved as carefully as family photos.

"You got yourself into this—don't expect me to bail you out!"

"If it weren't for you and your stupid ideas. . . ."

"Don't bother me. . . ."

Toxic emotional waste dumped into pure, inexperienced souls leaves a painful residue for years. Leftovers from devastated childhoods—insecurity, anger, rejection—can all contaminate our confidence as adults when going through crossroads. Sadly, we not only let our lethal legacy affect our lives and choices, we pass it on as a birthright to our own children. There they are, bright and shiny new, just waiting to receive their inheritance and we don't just pass it on—we dump it on them.

Families are not the only polluters of our emotional inner selves. We can allow ourselves to be driven by ambition, selfish motivation, and attachment to worldly pleasures. ("I can't get involved in that ministry, Lord. I'd have to give up my weekend work—and you know I'm saving up for that new . . .") Before we know it, we are really serving our every whim, while neglecting our deepest needs.

Power voices usually get their power from one source—fear. Fear makes us cling and control as if our lives depended on it. Fear tells us no one, not even God, can control our lives and situations better than we can.

Fear brings the lack of confidence we feel. And no seminar or book on "how to be confident" can help us change if fear of change has dug a deep trench in our soul.

Sadly, the most powerful of all the power voices are destructive things we say to ourselves. We believe the lies, and we exaggerate them, polluting our spirits and minds. Using a megaphone of negative *self-talk*, we reinforce deadly words we've heard about ourselves. And so we feed our own spirits with counter-productive ideas:

"I'm never going to make it. . . ."

"I can't do this. . . ."

"I shouldn't even waste my time trying. It won't do any good anyway."

"Given a fifty-fifty chance, I will make the wrong choice every time."

"It's my own fault I got myself into this. I can't possibly ask God to help me out."

If this is your problem, you are plundering your own future by inviting the poison of the past to take over and ruin your life. We can keep on destroying ourselves, or we can silence those voices, knowing that our God is the God of a new start and a second chance.

Is there rest from the voices that want to sabotage our lives? Before we can move on in our lives, we need to call in a specialist—someone who can help clean up the emotional dump and undo the spiritual traps.

We need not a power voice—but *the Voice of Power*. The Voice of ageless eternity. The same voice that whispered in softness to a young woman and brought love to earth in the form of a little baby.

> Be still before the LORD, all mankind, because He has roused himself from His holy dwelling.[1]
> But the LORD is in His holy temple; let all the earth be silent before Him.[2]

[1]Zechariah 2:13.
[2]Habakkuk 2:20.

Has there ever been a voice like God's? Is there a voice any-where that can stand up to His? Confront the power voices in your life and ask them, "Can your voice thunder like His?"[3]

> The voice of the LORD is over the waters; the God of glory thunders, the LORD thunders over the mighty waters. The voice of the LORD is powerful; the voice of the LORD is majestic. The voice of the LORD breaks the cedars; the LORD breaks in pieces the cedars of Lebanon. . . . The voice of the LORD strikes with flashes of lightning. The voice of the LORD shakes the desert. . . . The voice of the LORD twists the oaks and strips the forests bare. And in His tem-ple all cry, "Glory!" The LORD sits enthroned over the flood; the LORD is enthroned as King forever. The LORD gives strength to His people; the LORD blesses His people with peace.[4]

Listen to what God, *the* Power Voice would say to the voices that have been seizing control in your life.

> God has numbered the days of your reign and brought it to an end.[5]

The Lord wants to relieve you of the pressure and release you from the harassment of the voices you have listened to far too long.

He speaks words of comfort and courage, healing and love. His words are words of creativity and worth, immortality and life. He speaks words of strength, purpose, and victory.

> The weapons we fight with are not the weapons of the world. On the contrary, they have divine power to demol-ish strongholds. We demolish arguments and every pre-tension that sets itself up against the knowledge of God, and we take captive every thought to make it obedient to Christ.[6]

Will you believe His words?

> Here I am! I stand at the door and knock. If anyone hears my voice and opens the door, I will come in and eat

---

[3]Job 40:9b.
[4]Psalm 29:3–11.
[5]Daniel 5:26.
[6]2 Corinthians 10:4–5.

with him, and he with me.[7]

God wants not only to silence the voices competing for power in your life He wants to speak to you—definitely and directly—about the decisions and choices that lie ahead.

> Whether you turn to the right or to the left, your ears will hear a voice behind you, saying, "This is the way; walk in it."[8]

When we listen to God's voice, rising with authority above all the others, we can safely take the next step. Then we will have the foundation of trust and confidence because we will know it is *God* who has spoken. Will you listen? Or do you want to be stuck repeating the same old patterns in your life, without real growth or change? It's your decision—you might even say, a crossroads decision.

---

[7]Revelation 3:20.
[8]Isaiah 30:21.

# 7

# Identity in Christ

---

### Secret #6

### You can know who you are in Christ.

---

Statistics show four out of five American adults describe themselves as Christians. Would you believe that 60 to 65 million adults testify to having made a personal commitment to Christ and believe they will go to heaven because they have accepted Jesus Christ as their Savior?[1]

If this is true, why is there such a problem in our society directly related to the *decline* of Christian standards and influence? Could it be that, though many identify themselves as *Christians*, far fewer identify themselves with *Christ*?

Identifying yourself as a Christian is not the same as finding your identity in Christ. There is a vast difference between living *for* Christ, and living *in* Him—a sharp contrast between

---

[1]"The Church Today: Insightful Statistics and Commentary," Barna Research Group, Glendale, Calif., 1990.

living the *lifestyle* and living the *life*, between *professing* faith and *practicing* faith.

It may be true that many Christians are in the throes of an identity crisis of some kind. How can we be certain of anything in regard to character, goals, and decision if we have no sense of what defines us as a Christian person?

Those who experience an identity crisis live day to day, handling the routine and sudden events that happen in every life with no larger frame of reference to give perspective and objectivity. The varied, seemingly accidental events slam into the insecure identity, leaving the uncertain man or woman scrambling to manage as best they know how.

Those believers who have not taken the time to firmly establish their identity in Christ can experience difficulty in becoming mature members of the body of Christ and society. Dependent on others, they have difficulty establishing roles and moral boundaries. They run into constant snags in relationships and struggle with making decisions. Just navigating the normal crossroads—let alone more challenging ones—is overwhelming. It is like living as a missing person—or like a person who has pieces missing.

Searching for identity, some are even drawn back into the world's ways of solving an identity crisis. Drugs, money, sex, material things, power, influence, and position are all places many search to find meaning and the security of a whole identity.

Even as Christians, we can continue to try to solve an identity crisis by searching for and trying to fit into a mold that was never meant for us. If we are not careful, we model ourselves after each other, and instead of becoming like Christ, we just become like each other—reproductions, not originals; carbon-copy Christians. We learn to act the way we see others act.

How sad when our lives lack *authenticity*. How tragic when we can talk and act convincingly like Christians—yet there remains a void within that cannot be filled with Christian activity or commitment. It's a thirst only Christ can fill, a hunger only He can satisfy, and an identity crisis He alone can solve.

There is no greater need in the lives of believers than to know their identity in Christ. There can be no greater joy than to discover who you are in Christ. Realizing that they are wholly joined, tapped into his power, and easily moved by His influence is what makes ordinary people into successful cross-roads navigators. For when we are connected to Christ, it is in Him alone that we live and move. We become so grounded in Him that He is the basis for our being.

Such a life is a picture of intimate relationship with Christ, and it gives strength and blessing.

As long as we are ignorant of who we are in Christ, we can easily be kept enslaved. If we believe a lie about our identity based on our past, our failures, or our inabilities, we will continue to live in bondage and not as free children of God.

Many of our struggles and defeats are nothing more than the result of being ignorant of our identity in Christ. These defeats are especially acute in times when we need to move on, make goals, and take steps toward becoming what God has destined us to become.

Knowing who you are in Christ turns the tables on circumstances. When you come to a crossroads—even upheaval and major change—you can define the crossroads and not let it define you. Once you know who you are in Christ, you can know what to do when faced with crossroads decisions.

Let us illustrate further:

History-making advances have recently been made in genetic identification. Science is finding convincing evidence of ways in which individuals can be identified at the most basic level. Genetic profiles—sometimes called genetic fingerprints—can be as clearly identifiable as an actual fingerprint. These studies promise to establish identity with far more reliability than the conventional blood-type methods used previously.

Because of these scientific advances, health can be restored to victims of serious diseases, and even human history can be reconstructed from fragments of ancient bone or tissue. Wherever nucleated cells are found, a DNA or genetic fingerprint possibility exists. Deep within the animated network of a cell nucleus lies the molecule, the imprinted code that sets an individual apart from all others. The identification implications are nothing less than revolutionary. Psalm 139 begins to take on a whole new meaning when we read it in light of this scientific discovery:

> For you created my inmost being; you knit me together
> in my mother's womb. I praise you because I am fearfully

and wonderfully made; your works are wonderful, I know that full well. My frame was not hidden from you when I was made in the secret place. When I was woven together in the depths of the earth, your eye saw my unformed body.[2]

This same Creator—who was present at your conception—stamped His trademark deep in the molecular structure of your body. Even more than that, deep within your spirit there is God's touch—His trademark. It is a crucial place stamped with His image. This "spiritual genetic code" is God's trademark within the spirit of each person who has given their life to Him. Those who have accepted Jesus Christ are marked—identified in Christ.

It is because of our identity in Christ that we experience freedom from condemnation (Romans 8:1). It is the basis of our release from the power of sin, the liberation from the tyranny of self and being loosed from the chains of addictions and destructive habits. It is in our identification in Christ that we know firsthand what it means to be emancipated from the past, to be delivered from disadvantaged beginnings and escape the prisons of our personal defeats and regrets.

In Christ we are proven to be sons, not slaves. We are free to discover who we are, not depend on what we do. We are certified heirs, not outcasts. In Christ we are called to a purpose, not driven by emptiness. In Christ we are justified, glorified overcomers. We become those full of hope—victors. In Jesus Christ we become vessels of God's grace and wisdom.

In Christ we are being made totally new,[3] we are put into His processing plant, being re-created and rebuilt into that which was stolen from us as far back as Adam. In Christ we are His workmanship,[4] undergoing a transformation process in which He is working, He is shaping and molding, changing us for His purposes to meet His specifications and blueprints.

It is in Christ and our identity in Him that we are enabled to live a new life.[5] In Christ we are renewed[6] because of His working within. Our identity in Christ assures us that we are His possession, dead to sin and living for and in God.

---

[2]Psalm 139:13–16.
[3]2 Corinthians 5:17.
[4]Ephesians 2:8–10
[5]Romans 6:1–13.
[6]Colossians 3:3, 10–14.

And, it is in Christ that we are blessed without boundary or limit with every spiritual blessing.[7]

You can face the crossroads before you as the genuine, real-life *in Christ* believer that you are. An honest-to-goodness child of God, facing life realistically as a proven family-of-God member. You have a valid identification badge, stamped within your spirit—it is His own image.

As Pastor Jack Hayford says, "Image is not just a look. It's a design of thought. It's a pattern of values. Image is not just the surface layering—what we look like—it's substantive stuff. It touches the core of our being."[8]

Once we grasp hold of the power behind knowing our identity in Christ, every crossroads decision will be deeply affected. Every choice we make, every direction we choose—is an image issue. It is the very fabric of our character and a key determining factor in our future.

You may have been identified as many things, good or bad, before you became a Christian. Now you are a new creation, holding as much potential to become like Christ as a newborn has to become a strong, mature man or woman.

You may have hesitated at crossroads decisions before, but now the only hesitation you will make will be to check your identification and wait for directions. Crossroads choices no longer need to pose the problems they once did. They are present opportunities to show your legitimacy as a child of the Living God.

You, my friend, are a certified, credentialed *in Christ* believer. And should we ever meet in person, we'd probably know each other. You see, we carry the same identification—stamped with His image and signature. We belong not only to Him but also to each other. We're family! And if our spiritual DNA were to be checked—it would be identical, for it would be drawn from Immanuel's veins. His blood has given us the same new identity.

---

[7]Ephesians 1:3.
[8]Jack Hayford, *A Man's Image and Identity* (Living Way Ministries, 1993).

# 8

# God With Us

---

### Secret #7

**God sees, hears, and feels with us. His name is Immanuel—"God with us" is a daily experience, not merely a historical, biblical fact.**

---

Perhaps you've heard these lines before from unbelieving friends: "This Christian stuff is a bunch of baloney." "How could a loving God let such terrible things happen?" "How could a just God restrain himself in the face of the evil that blatantly parades itself in our world?" "How can He help but come with judgment and vengeance?" "Why doesn't the Almighty use His power to stop the evil wave of destruction and devastation of human suffering?" "If Jesus really came to earth to set up His kingdom, why does it feel as if we're living in the devil's workshop?"

If you're like most of us, you have secretly asked those

same questions, probably more than once. If not those, then how about these:

"If I gave my life to Christ, then why doesn't He just take charge and tell me what to do?" "Why doesn't God just re-program me to do what He wants? Why do I have to ask for direction with every decision I have to make?" "Why can't I make the decision to live His will once and for all—and have everything fall automatically into place after that?" "Since I have given my life to Him, why isn't the right decision obvious? Why do I have to struggle so?"

When help doesn't come the way we think it ought to come—what do we do then? Unfortunately, many resort to blaming God. Blame is based on a misconception of who God is, why He came, and why He came in the way that He did.

Jesus did not come into this world to *fix it*, though He has chosen to be involved in it. Our misconceptions about His purposes and chosen courses of action have caused misunderstanding from the very beginning.

## God With Us. . . .

Every Christmas, we hear the Scripture: "The virgin will be with child and will give birth to a son, and they will call Him Immanuel"—which means, "God with us."[1] Great news for a people who had been lost, hopeless, looking for God to send the Messiah—the One who would finally conquer and set up His kingdom.

However, it began to go wrong from the beginning.

Strangely enough, His arrival was not trumpeted to the populous, or announced within a gathering of the waiting, expecting faithful. Instead, on a regular afternoon, in the middle of a routine day, it was whispered to a young girl barely old enough to be considered a woman. When everyone was expecting Him—but when no one was looking for Him—He arrived in a most unusual manner, in a most repugnant place. Just as His coming was for a specific purpose, so was the *way* in which He came.

*He came into the reality of things as they were—to penetrate the human scene.*

He came to a world that was taxed beyond reason—a world

---
[1]Matthew 1:23.

so full of sin it had reached even the synagogue. He came when the world was too busy to notice and when worship was commercialized almost beyond recognition. The human scene is, tragically, much the same today.

But His *purpose* has not changed, nor have the people He has come to save. The front page of humanity's news is still filled with stories of pain and frustration. People are taxed by life and circumstances. And—still looking for a king—we would prefer one who was born *above* our painful station, not one born right into the middle of it.

Jesus—God with us—came to *enter* our world, not rescue it. Not to conquer, but to overcome. Not to take charge of the world, but to change it—one heart at a time.

*He came to touch you and enable you to touch your world. He came to make a difference.*

The Son of God knows, with heartfelt familiarity, the remote place in which you find yourself. He is still making himself available to come into the very drudgery of human hearts and lives.

No circumstances can restrict God's power from entering when the heart is willing and open. Jesus comes to where we live, to change things where we are—and He doesn't leave us to fend for ourselves.

The emotional struggle that saps the strength out of us is the very point where He can enter our lives to stay and heal. Circumstances that threaten to be our undoing—even if they have come *because* of our doing—is where He meets us and stays to see us through.

He comes into our sense of *insignificance* to see us through to lives of *purpose* and meaning.

He comes into our *defeat* and leads us to *victory.*

He comes into our *emptiness* and brings the *abundance* of His glorious presence.

## Wherever You Go—God Goes

"I am with you and will watch over you wherever you go, and I will bring you back to this land. I will not leave you until I have done what I have promised you."[2]

Wherever He sends you He goes.

---

[2]Genesis 28:15

"The LORD replied, 'My Presence will go with you, and I will give you rest.' Then Moses said to Him, 'If your Presence does not go with us, do not send us up from here. How will anyone know that you are pleased with me and with your people unless you go with us? What else will distinguish me and your people from all the other people on the face of the earth?' And the LORD said to Moses, 'I will do the very thing you have asked, because I am pleased with you and I know you by name.' "[3]

Whatever you battle—He battles:

"When you go to war against your enemies and see horses and chariots and an army greater than yours, do not be afraid of them, because the LORD your God, who brought you up out of Egypt, will be with you."[4]

Whatever you face—He faces:

"When you pass through the waters, I will be with you; and when you pass through the rivers, they will not sweep over you. When you walk through the fire, you will not be burned; the flames will not set you ablaze."[5]

Whatever you feel—He feels:

"For we do not have a high priest who is unable to sympathize with our weaknesses, but we have one who has been tempted in every way, just as we are—yet was without sin."[6]

Whenever you meet—He comes:

"For where two or three come together in my name, there am I with them."[7]

Whatever He asks—He enables:

"Therefore go and make disciples of all nations, baptizing them in the name of the Father and of the Son and of the Holy Spirit, and teaching them to obey everything I have commanded you. And surely I am with you always, to the very end of the age."[8]

## Will You Go With God?

"O LORD, you have searched me and you know me. You know when I sit and when I rise; you perceive my thoughts

---

[3]Exodus 33:14–17.
[4]Deuteronomy 20:1.
[5]Isaiah 43:2.
[6]Hebrews 4:15.
[7]Matthew 18:20
[8]Matthew 28:19–20.

from afar. You discern my going out and my lying down; you are familiar with all my ways. Before a word is on my tongue you know it completely, O LORD. You hem me in—behind and before; you have laid your hand upon me. Such knowledge is too wonderful for me, too lofty for me to attain.

"Where can I go from your Spirit? Where can I flee from your presence? If I go up to the heavens, you are there; if I make my bed in the depths, you are there. If I rise on the wings of the dawn, if I settle on the far side of the sea, even there your hand will guide me, your right hand will hold me fast.

"If I say, 'Surely the darkness will hide me and the light become night around me,' even the darkness will not be dark to you; the night will shine like the day, for darkness is as light to you.

"For you created my inmost being; you knit me together in my mother's womb. I praise you because I am fearfully and wonderfully made; your works are wonderful, I know that full well. My frame was not hidden from you when I was made in the secret place. When I was woven together in the depths of the earth, your eyes saw my unformed body. All the days ordained for me were written in your book before one of them came to be.

"How precious to me are your thoughts, O God! How vast is the sum of them! Were I to count them, they would outnumber the grains of sand. When I awake, I am still with you."[9]

Wherever the enemy is attacking—He is with us. Wherever relationships are fractured—He is with us. Wherever home and marriages are shattered—He is with us. Hassled, hurried, irritated, exasperated believer—God is with you. Immanuel is His name.

Yes, it's true. He didn't come to change the world—but each of us. To forgive so we would live life as forgiven people. To heal us so we can approach life as whole people. To love us, so we can love. He came to make a difference in us, to enable us to make a difference in our world. He doesn't change history—but through us, He makes history. And He came to do the same, in and through you.

If we really believed that God was with us each minute of every day, how would we change? How would our lives change? How differently would we approach the crossroads

---

[9]Psalm 139:1–18.

experiences that come to all of us?

Yes, it appears that successful crossroads navigators do know certain secrets. They face the milestone moments of their individual lives armed with those secrets. They know the difference between a crisis and a crossroads, they know why they pray and how to pray. They know that prayer is more about relationship than requests. They have learned to identify and listen to God's voice. The secrets they share include not just knowing who they are in Christ, but Who He is in them. And they know Him by name—Immanuel. Secrets that you now know, too.

And knowing these steps is only the beginning. In order to safely complete your passage through a crossroads you will also need to make certain choices.

In Section Two we will examine some of the most important choices you may ever make in your life.

# *Part Two*

## Successful Crossroads Navigators Come to Terms Quickly With Important Choices

# 9

# It's in the Bag

---

### Choice #1

### Choose to get rid of excess
### emotional baggage.

---

Perhaps you have witnessed this scene: Loaded with too many suitcases and carry-ons, the breathless passenger barely makes the flight. Pushing inside the totally booked plane, he proceeds to bump and jostle everyone around him as he stows his bags—much to everyone's annoyance.

The luggage we cart onto the crowded plane is as troublesome as the "inner baggage" that can weigh us down, and drag us to a complete stop, just when we need to move ahead with God in courage. Emotional luggage that encumbers our decisions and entangles us in sin is what hinders us from serving God with happy abandon. These old emotions cause us to be indecisive, ineffective, and unable to carry out what we know God has promised or given us to do. And we need to address those issues as so much excess baggage:

"Let us throw off everything that hinders and the sin that

so easily entangles, and let us run with perseverance the race marked out for us."[1]

This word isn't just for those who are facing tough times or persecution. It's for those who would say, "I seem to be banging my head against a brick wall when it comes to making decisions. And I need a sure foundation, a solid base—stability when everything seems to be up in the air waiting for me to make my decision." It is a powerful word. *Don't give up! Hang in there! Don't quit now!*

It is in the midst of the confusing options that comes a gentle, loving word from God: *Lay down your excess baggage.*

Can you picture a man running through the airport, loaded with baggage and trying to catch his flight? Now can you imagine that he is not headed for a plane, but competing in an athletic event—say, running hurdles? The TV camera crew zooms in on the competitors. There in the arena the athletes line up waiting for the starting signal. The stands are full of enthusiastic fans and friends. The hurdles are placed around the course—a specially designed and difficult course. In addition to the normal and standard hurdles, the runners will be expected to also navigate around or jump over obstacles that may be thrown in front of them at any moment. There are the runners now, decked out in the most expensive running shoes, trunks, and tank tops, numbers blaring from their chests—and carrying two or three full suitcases.

What we have just given you is a mental picture of life!

Unable to escape from it, unable to guard against it—life happens. And, when it gets challenging, we may try to numb ourselves in order to tolerate it, drug ourselves to avoid it, or entertain ourselves in an effort to delay it. But eventually we have to face the fact—it's our life and we have to live it—the racetrack is a one-way street. We entered, and we will finish, one way or another.

Filled with all kinds of challenges, obstacles, and adversities—life can get really hard. Someday we will be facing heaven—wonderful, peaceful heaven. But for now we face life. We need to be equipped, and ready to run the race with endurance, without stumbling and falling down. We run a race that is punctuated with crossroads experiences, requiring good decision-making skills and courage—because the race is

---

[1]Hebrews 12:1.

full of unexpected turns of events, sudden challenges, unannounced situations requiring quick decisions, difficult to handle.

Ted Roberts from Gresham, Oregon, told a conference of pastors the story about how he always wanted to ride a speed bike, one of those *tour de France* types. When he bought the bike the salesman told him, "Man, this is so fast, you'll see yourself going by. You think you're ready for this?"

"Now this was not the kind of bike you just go out and buy, get on, and ride home," Ted explained. "You don't just get on this bike, you clip your feet to the pedals. Furthermore, you don't just get off this bike without knowing how." Ted took his bike home and without reading the instruction manual he went for a ride. He made his way up into the Cascade Mountains. He began to navigate the roadway easily, taking each curve with ease and speed—lots of speed.

"I'm doing great," he said to himself. Then he came around a right curve and headlong toward a group of tourists standing on a bridge, blocking the road. He hit the brakes, came to a complete stop—suddenly remembering that his feet were clipped to the pedals. *Wham!* He fell sideways. The quick-thinking tourists seized the opportunity and began taking pictures. Lying on the ground in a tangle, feeling like an idiot, he realized how crucial it is to be ready for whatever is around the corner. For him, it meant knowing how to unclip his feet from the bike pedals in an emergency.

We all need to learn a lesson from Ted. It's dangerous to start out unprepared for the unexpected. We need to know how to untangle from things that have entangled us.

We don't believe for a moment that the triumphant life is completely free of difficulty or obstacles—just the opposite. But those who are triumphant on a daily basis are those who face the difficulties of life with a different dynamic. They make right choices because they allow the Word of God to change the way they define circumstances and the way they handle challenges.

People who triumph have also come to terms with the fact that winning means you learn to streamline. If you are to run your race victoriously, it's time to get rid of those things that weigh you down—the excess baggage you carry.

Where does all that baggage come from anyway? Why do we try to run the race all weighted down like that?

Excess baggage often comes from the same places the "toxic waste" we mentioned earlier comes from. For example, there may be baggage inherited from an alcoholic parent or a driven parent. You may not have inherited the alcoholism, but what about your need to control, or to do things just right, or your fear of risk and exposure to failure? What about "spend-aholism"? Or "escapism"? Perfectionism can drive us with insatiable strivings, demanding that we produce more and better. Performance-based individuals, who find their identity in doing, are denied the joy of just *being.* They carry baggage that is stuffed full of unreachable goals, unreasonable expectations, and rigid schedules carefully planned to reach those goals. No, they may not be alcoholics or workaholics, but they have carried on a family tradition just the same.

Then there's the baggage of *peer pressure* you gave in to way back in high school. Making every effort to fit in and be a part may have led you into habits you cannot quit. To make compromises you can't correct. Guilt gets stuffed into this bag.

There is also the baggage of *insecurity,* the need to be controlled and have someone else make the decisions for us because we weren't trained in making decisions. If you were never encouraged in a caring way to make choices on your own, insecurity can be like excess baggage that you carry for a lifetime. Insecurity feeds on an overgrown awareness of inadequacies and imperfections. And the insecurity can have a matching piece of baggage—known as the *importance*, or *ego* bag. In it, we drag along our inflated sense of importance. We carry in this bag our accomplishments, our slightly inflated resumé, right beside our diplomas and degrees, next to the achievement awards and badges. The ego bag also has an outside pocket where we keep our opinions. It's essential to have them handy should someone ever want to discuss anything, on any topic. It's the bag that you hold out whenever you think you might be mistaken for someone ordinary—all the while afraid someone might discover that you are.

There is also the bag you fill up with traumatic events and tragic memories of abuse or abandonment. Pictures of our disappointment are kept in a resentment album inside that suitcase, as are incidences of incest, molestation, emotional and verbal abuse. Even though this bag is so wearisome and heavy, stuffed beyond its capacity, we can always find room to store one more painful disaster.

One suitcase that is dragged around day by day—the real tattered-looking one, held together with tape and gauze—is the "hurts" bag. All the people who have ever caused hurt feelings are in this bag. That junior high school teacher who embarrassed you in front of the whole class, that lady who accused you wrongfully, that boyfriend or girlfriend who stood you up instead of accompanying you to the senior prom—all these are stuffed into the "hurts" bag.

Tragically, we get so used to carrying these pieces of excess baggage, we don't even know that other people are aware that we're loaded with extra baggage. They notice our overload and offer to help us carry our bags, they may even try to convince us to lay down the baggage—but we don't understand what they are saying and question their motives. Pride makes us afraid they will tell someone what they saw in our bags. So we guard our baggage and hold on to it tighter.

The truth is, the bags are getting heavier and heavier. We find an easily accessible outside pocket on one of our bags, where we keep a supply of "emotional trading stamps." What do these do for us? They allow us to say, "Because I have this heavy, terrible, and awkward thing in my life, I cannot be asked to or expected to change. . . ."

We trade in self-protection and compromise. We give away freedom and growth.

## More Baggage

And of course there is an anger bag. It's where we keep the insults we save to spit at inconsiderate people in our lives. We save up explosions for our children or parents. We keep this bag close and handy—we use it most often.

There is also an unforgiveness bag, which we never open, except to stuff in another offense.

Then there is the "spiritual" bag—where we tuck every issue we'd rather avoid or deny. "God's taking care of it," we say. We don't have any problems, we boast—that is, of course, as long we can pack them in this bag. We criticize others for having problems, for carrying them right out in the open.

## Put It Down

You may laugh at this silly illustration. But, really, isn't it time to get rid of the excess bags? Wouldn't it be wonderful to be free of fear, guilt, anger, mistrust, insecurity, unforgiveness and all the rest of the excess emotional and spiritual weights? Aren't you tired of being kept from running your race—or being prevented from making it through your crossroads?

We are not so different from you. We, too, struggle occasionally with baggage and find that we've picked up emotional weights again and again. We, too, find ourselves being tripped up with anger, disappointment, and being disgusted with ourselves.

The message of this chapter is simply that God has a wonderful way of exposing our baggage—of spilling the contents out in such a manner that we are sometimes forced to look at all we've stuffed and packed away. He longs to show us a better way to live, and when we choose at last to look at the inner contents of our souls, it will make us wonder why we've taken such effort to carry our excess baggage so long. We've learned that God won't let us continue to smooth or gloss over our excess emotional baggage with excuses, blaming everyone else because we are weighted down.

*They are our bags.*

We have found that no one is going to carry these bags for us. We can't park them on the back porch and ignore them. The trash collector will not conveniently cart them off. *We* have to get rid of these life-draining weights. And to do that, *we have to give them away.*

To get rid of spiritually hindering baggage we have to give it all to God. That means going to the foot of the cross in prayer and abandoning all the excess baggage.

Picture yourself again as the man at the airport. This time you can check it all at the counter—never to carry it again. The Savior is there to take your bags. But we must warn you: He's going to ship them away—not on the plane you've come to catch, but on an aircraft headed in the exact opposite direction, toward a destination that is as far away as the east is from the west. And when the plane is over just the right spot, He will drop every one of them into the deepest sea. And you will finally be free.

Free to make the decisions you need to make without being encumbered and without hindrance. Free to walk on with confidence, taking one more step as you navigate your crossroads.

If we are ever going to run the race, jump the hurdles, and

navigate the obstacles and barriers that life throws in our pathway, we need to trim down our load—to get rid of all the unnecessary extra hindrances and be able to finish the race with energy to spare. God wants to do something special in each of us—we can be different—before we get to the other side of our crossroads experience. Will we give Him our excess baggage?

Why not take some time right now to unload your baggage and see what you've been carrying so long—and what's been weighing you down? Pray, and offer it to Christ. Let Him take it away and give you His strength to go on.

He will.

# 10

# Living Today

---

### Choice #2

**Choose to put the past in the past—not
to forget, but to use and learn from it.**

---

Perhaps you have been wondering what the last couple of chapters have to do with facing life's crossroads.

Why check for toxic waste? Why lose your old baggage? What has our emotional makeup got to do with our ability to make decisions as we face our many and varied crossroads experiences?

We think these issues are crucial and must be addressed. So before we go on, we'd like to make a few connections—to put the last few chapters in perspective, and show how they are essential as you successfully face and safely navigate your crossroads experiences. Our goal is to help you to realize that inability to make godly, wise decisions may have its cause in the foundation of what and who you are. We want to help you see the value of being able to adopt a philosophy of life based securely on something other than your personal history. This book is about finding a new you—and helping you rebuild on a new foundation, giving you the ability to look forward, rather than basing every decision on what is behind—in the past.

It's important to understand that often we're still affected by those who have given us excess emotional baggage or stuffed items into it. In fact, it is crucial to understand how we are still affected if we are to rebuild life from the foundation up.

Evidence of a life that has been built on a *faulty* foundation is apparent when we choose to live in an *opposite* or *reverse* attitude. We will illustrate what we mean by this with a brief anecdote:

There was a mother who reacted intensely against the way she was raised and purposely did everything just the opposite of what her mother did to her. For example, her mother determined what she ate, what she wore, who her friends were, where she went to college, and what she would study there. Her mother dictated her every move, dominated her every thought and opinion. Her decisions were completely controlled, if not dictated.

When the woman was grown and married—to a man of her mother's choice—she had a daughter. It was then she decided something for herself. She would be a different kind of mother. She allowed her daughter every freedom. The daughter picked out her own clothes from the time she was old enough to point. She was never encouraged to eat anything she didn't like. Every friend her daughter selected was accepted without question. The daughter grew up and went to the college she chose, and transferred classes if she didn't like the teacher. The woman never forced or even shared her personal opinions with her daughter—all in reaction to the way her own mother raised her. The daughter never had a curfew, or any restrictions on activities. There was no interference in her schoolwork, no influence on her decisions.

The plan backfired. The woman eventually concluded, "I now have a daughter who is just like my mother."

## Let's Look at It

How much are you reacting to the way you were raised? Do you have such a strong commitment to being different that you are in danger of making the same mistake this woman made—overcompensating, so that you just make different big mistakes? Unfortunately, the "sins of the fathers" can in a very real sense be passed on this way, even when the exact opposite is our goal.[1]

In the same way, when facing crossroads, we may react to an indecisive parent by being impulsive—thinking all the while that we aren't going to make the same mistakes of the weak parent who couldn't make up his mind or make a decision. Perhaps we were so victimized by the impulsive decisions of a parent that we made a vow to be more careful and responsible—except that now we never really know when to make a move or a decision. It is possible to become as indecisive as our parents were impulsive.

I'm sure you can see that making a decision will take being free from the unhealthy influences of the past. If you are one of the fortunate ones who was raised by skillful and loving parents, you may have a foundation in your life that is strong. So many do not have this foundation. The Bible promises that we can rebuild a spiritual foundation in which God can direct us, at the same time ending family instability, ". . . showing love to a thousand generations of those who love me and keep my commandments."[2]

Yes, it's true, we can know His mercy *and* pass it on. "His mercy extends to those who fear Him, from generation to generation."[3] Not only can we clean out the unhealthy baggage in our own lives, we can pass on a new spiritual heritage to our children:

"O my people, hear my teaching; listen to the words of my mouth. I will open my mouth in parables, I will utter hidden things, things from of old—what we have heard and known, what our fathers have told us. We will not hide them from their children; we will tell the next generation the praiseworthy deeds of the LORD, His power, and the wonders He has done."[4]

How wonderful to know the reality of God's love and goodness—and to have it impact our most important decisions, to pass it on to our families! "For the LORD is good and His love

---

[1]Exodus 20:5.
[2]Exodus 20:6.
[3]Luke 1:50.
[4]Psalm 78:1–4.

endures forever; His faithfulness continues through all generations."[5]

Here is good news for those who would unplug from the control panel of the past:

"The Spirit of the Sovereign LORD is on me, because the LORD has anointed me to preach good news to the poor. He has sent me to bind up the brokenhearted, to proclaim freedom for the captives and release from darkness for the prisoners, to proclaim the year of the LORD's favor and the day of vengeance of our God, to comfort all who mourn, and provide for those who grieve in Zion—to bestow on them a crown of beauty instead of ashes, the oil of gladness instead of mourning, and a garment of praise instead of a spirit of despair. They will be called oaks of righteousness, a planting of the LORD for the display of His splendor. They will rebuild the ancient ruins and restore the places long devastated; they will renew the ruined cities that have been devastated for generations."[6]

Philippians 2:15 says it this way:

" . . . so that you may become blameless and pure, children of God without fault in a crooked and depraved generation, in which you shine like stars in the universe."

We can discover a totally new way to live!

"Therefore, brothers, since we have confidence to enter the Most Holy Place by the blood of Jesus, by a new and living way opened for us through the curtain, that is, His body, and since we have a great priest over the house of God, let us draw near to God with a sincere heart in full assurance of faith, having our hearts sprinkled to cleanse us from a guilty conscience and having our bodies washed with pure water. Let us hold unswervingly to the hope we profess, for He who promised is faithful."[7]

Can you imagine having the strength and courage to be able to make decisions without wavering, basing them on a new and living way—on faithful promises instead of unfaithful human reasoning, past failures, or excess emotional baggage? Think of the freedom to be able to take new steps, depending on God's *reliability* and His *trustworthiness*. Imagine confidence in God replacing fear, anger, and insecurity. Imagine being able to persevere with promise, knowing that God is for

---

[5]Psalm 100:5.
[6]Isaiah 61:1–4.
[7]Hebrews 10:19–23.

you instead of fearfully stumbling through, hoping we're do-ing the right thing . . . hoping for the best, but really expecting the worst. "You need to persevere so that when you have done the will of God, you will receive what He has promised."[8]

How would your life change if you knew for sure that God alone holds your reward, that from Him only comes the very essence of your life? What if you could be free from having to be in total control or having to take charge of your own life and destiny, barreling through crossroads with no regard for those who depend on you to make good decisions?

Come to your merciful Father God, and let Him show you how to rebuild your broken foundations. Let Him unplug you from the control board others have used to control you. Open yourself before Him, and let Him heal those broken places that form weak foundations in you. In faith, we can know He re-ceives us when we come, *and* He gives us the courage and strength to remove the corruption of unforgiveness from our hearts. With His help, we can accept that the people who have polluted our lives with toxic waste and excess baggage had no idea what they were doing when they used us to meet their own emotional needs.

When this occurs, our false needs and pretenses can come down. Instead of struggling with a puzzle that is too big for us to see, we can begin to rest and let God show us where *all* the pieces fit, not just the pretty ones. We can stand at the fork-in-the-road, ready to receive direction, wanting a fresh start, with hope and courage.

Can you see it? One of the options each crossroads expe-rience presents is to continue just the same as we are—loaded with lies and overloaded with injury and pain. Or we can be-gin to walk on a new, living roadway of wholeness and free-dom. The one is wide and makes room for all our excess bag-gage. It provides plenty of room for us to continue carrying our oversized loads of individual failures, independent attitudes, and destructive self-talk. But, the new and living way is nar-row—as narrow as the cross of Calvary. It will only accom-modate those who are willing to put down all the baggage of the old *self* life.

This is scary footing, to be sure! Even though the first steps are faltering, they are *your* steps—taken on free and secure

---

[8]Hebrews 10:36.

ground in Christ. Though it may not feel like it now, you will soon be able to take some steadier steps as your life becomes more deeply rooted in a personal and intimate relationship with Christ, founded securely on His Word.

You see, the choice made right here will affect *all* the crossroads choices you will face for the rest of your life. It's a choice no one can make for another—it's a personal choice, yours alone to make.

How about it? Are you ready to leave behind the old independent *self*—to let go and allow God to resurrect you into a new life?

Ask Him to help you. He is waiting.

# 11

# Rebuilding From the Ground Up

---

### Choice #3

**Choose to repair and/or rebuild the
foundations of your life.**

---

It can be difficult to lay down baggage we've accumulated
from the past. In a way, it has kept our life in balance. Once
the baggage is unloaded, it can leave you feeling a little un-
steady. Standing unsure on shaky ground is very frightening.
(We know. We live in California.)

Even if you haven't experienced an earthquake firsthand,
we have all experienced emotional rumblings from time to
time.

In the last few chapters we have been very clear about how
important we think it is to live life on a steady foundation. In
fact, we've taken several chapters to illustrate how many suffer damage far beneath the surface. Furthermore, when a per-

son stands at a crossroads needing to make a decision—*even if all the options are positive*—any change can shake her life and threaten all that she has learned to depend on. You may feel paralyzed and unable to choose.

If that isn't enough, we can experience several emotional aftershocks, so that the beliefs on which we have grounded our lives continue to shift beneath us. In our spirits, it can feel as though the ground we stand on is crumbling. Life is uncertain, that's for sure. But we have good news.

In the physical world, an earthquake can leave all your possessions in a heap. But it doesn't have to be that way emotionally or spiritually. Even if it seems as if all is crumbling around you, there is a way to "quake-proof" your life.

Earthquakes and *lifequakes* have one thing in common: Irrespective of construction, anything standing on loose soil or fill is vulnerable. One of the many stories coming out of the Los Angeles area, following the recent quake there, concerns a man who was determined to build his house on a particularly beautiful lot. It had a spectacular view of the city below, it was a nice neighborhood, and it was very expensive. When an architect looked at the selected home sight, however, he balked. He didn't like the geological surveyor's report. Underneath the pricy piece of real estate was a deep layer of sand. The homeowner insisted the faulty soil problem could be overcome and set about to have pilings cemented in—to sand. The architect quit. The determined homeowner proceeded. The story is one of wise advice ignored, warnings unheeded, and objections overruled with reason and manipulation. Then the contractor decided he didn't want his good reputation tied to such a risky project. Sub-contractors felt the same. The stubborn man, bent on having his house, found whomever he could to finish the ill-fated project. City hall was bombarded with requests for variances and exceptions to the building code. In the end the man got his house: expensive lighting, imported hand-painted tile, gold-plated fixtures, silk wall coverings and all. It was quite a showpiece—until January 1994. When the quake hit, the house fell in forty seconds. The trapped occupants had to dig their way through the rubble to safety. Except for the grandmother, who died in her bed.

How much are we like this man? We know what faulty foundations our lives are grounded on. So we try to make up for it—to compensate. We move our families as far away from our troubled beginnings as possible. We make every effort to build wonderful memories, maintain church involvement, and keep up with our neighbors. We construct lives in much the same way the man in L.A. built his house—with the finest of everything. And, even though we may have a lovely building, solid construction, and beautiful decor—if it is not standing on solid ground, it is vulnerable. And we know it.

Before you jump to wrong conclusions, we are not suggesting you ditch your jobs and families in an attempt to start over. Let's wait a minute. Your "house" may be okay—maybe it's just the foundation or footings that need work. Does that sound impossible?

A recent PBS show, about the salvation and repair of an old barn, said a lot to us about *spiritual restructuring* and what *is* possible with God.

## A Whole New House

Somewhere in a rural area of the northeast stood an old weathered barn looking quite unattractive and forlorn. But the property had a new owner who saw promise in the old structure, and decided it would make a charming home. By the time the TV viewers were brought in on the project, several decisions had already been made. Except for one large beam, the barn structure was deemed strong enough for the transformation. The plan called for a loft that would hold the weight of occupants and maybe a waterbed, which meant a weight-bearing beam would need to be replaced. Replacing the beam was the simplest part of the project. Much more serious was the crumbling foundation. It wouldn't hold the present building much longer, to say nothing of the planned refurbishing efforts.

It was most interesting to listen to the discussion as the men involved first inspected, then evaluated, and finally turned each problem into a possibility, every obstacle into a challenge. The house would simply need to be lifted off it's foundation, and a new foundation built underneath. Carpenters began stripping the building to it's barest, skeletal structure. Then they added bracing, reinforcing, and hammered extra support in place. A special crew was called in to lift the structure from its crumbling base. Construction workers were able to dig and remove decayed cement and stone. In the process, the stone buried within the decaying foundation was discovered to be of special value, because it was a rare native stone, too valuable to discard. Instead, it was cleaned and put into neat piles for reuse. With new footings dug, the cement was poured. Finally the useable stone was placed back in the foundation with new cement and reinforcing rods of iron for extra strength.

Slowly the structure was lowered onto it's "new" foundation. All this was possible for one reason. What was under the crumbling foundation—what kept it from collapsing even though the foundation had decayed—was *solid rock.* For years, though the foundation was faulty, it rested on solid ground, and was therefore able to hold the building up. Then the owner's new vision for the building could become a reality—something far greater than was ever perceived. It wasn't a barn any longer—it proceeded to become a lovely home, a place of shelter and fun and life. A home. Who would have ever guessed it could be?

It's hard not to compare the two illustrations: one, a lovely, expensive home built like it would stand forever, crumbled in less than forty seconds; the other an abandoned ruin, looking like it would fall at any moment—restored for more than a lifetime. Not only that, the barn became far more than it started out to be.

In both cases, doom and destiny were determined by what existed *underneath.*

The man in California preferred *geography,* or surface location and position over *geology,* the strata beneath. Unfortunately, he paid a dearer price than he ever expected to pay. The barn was based on *geology,* solid ground. It's *geography,* or location, was only important as it affected usefulness. The big house was doomed to fall; the barn was destined for a resurrected life—and with vision, it became something greater than anyone imagined.

Is it possible to become more than one has been perceived to be? *Yes!* Because God has a vision for each of us. Both of us (Neva and Zane) know what it's like to build solid structures in our lives, to taste success—and then have some "foundational" fault show up in need of repair work.

We believe the same for you. No matter what you've been told. No matter how you've been treated. Whether you've been an outward success and an inward failure—or just the opposite—it's not too late for you to have a foundational overhaul.

Your crossroads may be pointing out a "weight-bearing beam" that will need replacing if you are to become more than you are right now. But your life can be rebuilt from the ground up. And what's more, perhaps this is why you have picked up this book right at this time. The place you are in today—the crossroads you face—requires extra support. And it needs to come from beneath the surface—from the solid strata on which your life is built. What is that strata?

"He is like a man building a house, who dug down deep and laid the foundation on rock. When a flood came, the torrent struck that house but could not shake it, because it was well built."[1]

Life's unexpected surprises will come to the prepared and the unprepared. Will you be ready? Will your life become something that will stand for generations? Or will you be like the man in California, who would not listen to sound advice?

"But the one who hears my words and does not put them into practice is like a man who built a house on the ground without a foundation. The moment the torrent struck that house, it collapsed and its destruction was complete."[2]

Before you take another step, make another decision, or handle one more of life's surprises, God wants you to know this: *He alone can make you whole.* The foundations of your life *can* be put into good repair. And even when the weight of choices loads you down, God can help you find and replace the faulty, weak elements, the overstressed, "weight-bearing beams" in the structure of your life.

The promise He has for you today is the same one the psalmist knew:

"Though you have made me see troubles, many and bitter, you will restore my life again; from the depths of the earth you will again bring me up. You will increase my honor and comfort me once again."[3]

Even if your life lies in ruin around your feet, His Word begs you to trust Him for new things:

"Come, let us return to the LORD. He has torn us to pieces but He will heal us; He has injured us but He will bind up our wounds. After two days He will revive us; on the third day He

---

[1]Luke 6:48
[2]Luke 6:49
[3]Psalm 71:20–21

will restore us, that we may live in His presence. Let us acknowledge the LORD; let us press on to acknowledge Him. As surely as the sun rises, He will appear; He will come to us like the winter rains, like the spring rains that water the earth."[4]

God, the Creator of the universe, is also the Rebuilder of broken lives and the Repairer of faulty foundations:

" 'I will restore you to health and heal your wounds,' declares the LORD, 'because you are called an outcast, Zion for whom no one cares.' This is what the LORD says: 'I will restore the fortunes of Jacob's tents and have compassion on his dwellings; the city will be rebuilt on her ruins, and the palace will stand in its proper place.' "[5]

Like the new owner of the little barn-turned-palace, God sees the promise in you. He has a vision for you. He not only sees what you are but what you can become:

"They will say, 'This land that was laid waste has become like the garden of Eden; the cities that were lying in ruins, desolate and destroyed, are now fortified and inhabited.' Then the nations around you that remain will know that I the LORD have rebuilt what was destroyed and have replanted what was desolate. I the LORD have spoken, and I will do it."[6]

God doesn't make empty promises and boast egotistically. Everything He promises, He can produce.

"And God is able to make all grace abound to you, so that in all things at all times, having all that you need, you will abound in every good work."[7]

Afraid you'll not be able to make it? That even if God promises, *you* will fail? "To Him who is able to keep you from falling and to present you before His glorious presence without fault and with great joy—"[8]

You can probably see that we're absolutely serious about encouraging you to let God remake you from the inside. More importantly, so is God. He sees more in you than you could ever imagine. But before you can become all He wants you to be—all you *can* be—your life has to be solid, from the ground up. Will you let Him inspect your foundations? And afterward, will you let Him do the "groundwork" needed?

---

[4]Hosea 6:1–3
[5]Jeremiah 30:17–18
[6]Ezekiel 36:35–36
[7]2 Corinthians 9:8
[8]Jude 1:24

If so, it's time to take a giant step toward that crossroads you face. Time to stand on a solid foundation, free of the weight of excess baggage, with a mind and heart cleansed from the toxic waste of the past. Like the little child with the puzzle pieces, our decisions are lying face-up on the table before God.

It's time to start putting the picture together.

# 12

# Making Changes

---

### Choice #4

**Successful crossroads navigators have chosen to be open to the change and growth each crossroads experience offers.**

---

We raised several important questions at the beginning of this book: How do you face the tough decision and find the courage to examine your options, especially in the midst of turmoil? Is there really a way to make *good* decisions when standing at crossroads so crucial you must choose—knowing that to do nothing is as big a mistake as making the wrong choice?

We believe that each of us can learn to identify the crossroads as it approaches, clearly understand our options, and then make important decisions in such a way as to further the cause and purposes of God in our individual lives. And what we have attempted to do is to walk you through spiritual principles that will not only help you to make your life choices, but come to know God in a more intimate way than ever before.

So far, we have taken several positive, scripturally based steps through your crossroads already. You can:

☐ Use turning-point moments to choose new beginnings.
☐ Know the difference between a crossroads and a crisis.
☐ Pray, making God the center of your life—not your emotions.
☐ Know the power voices and learn to listen to the Voice of Power.
☐ Get rid of excess baggage.
☐ Put the past in the past.
☐ Rebuild from the ground up.

If you look over this list, you will see that every step is important and cannot be left out. If your crossroads can be pictured as a stream—and the steps you've taken so far are stepping-stones to help you get across—you'd now be approaching the middle. This is not the time to walk away from the process, saying, "I've got the hang of this now. I can do it from here by myself."

The stream is deep, and the water is cold!

Even though we speak from personal experience as well as from the stories of the people we frequently counsel, you may want to turn back to old habits of self-determination. In today's versions of Christianity, it is easy to think that God is here just for your comfort and not to direct you. In fact, He can allow things to get *un*comfortable so that He can more easily direct.

If you step away from the process now, you may find yourself as confused and non-directed as ever. Why? Because you need to take the next step: *Let the crossroads change you.*

This requires a change in viewpoint: It is time to accept that a crossroads is not a problem, but a *place*. Change is not a permanent condition, but a passing opportunity. While we are busy trying to make a decision, we may be missing a moment of discovery.

The richness of life is most often found *on the way*, along the *journey*—while we are looking for answers. As we have seen, we can use the time productively.

Once we discover that life is a spiritual journey as well as an outward journey, we learn that, much of the time, we get focused on the wrong problem—we focus on outward circumstances, when that is not the only matter we need to face.

Maybe you've had the experience of visiting with a pastor to talk about a problem with your teenager. To your surprise—and perhaps irritation—the pastor asks about your own insecurities and fear of failure.

You think, *This is not why I came. It's my kid!* Yes, it is true if the teenager doesn't get his act together it will make us appear not to have our act together. That would be embarrassing, wouldn't it? But we don't want to deal with the fact that our perfectionism and need to control may be a part of the young person's problem.

Sometimes when a woman seeks counsel concerning the lack she sees in her husband, it becomes uncomfortable when the counselor suggests they talk, not about the husband—but the relationship. Suddenly the conversation gets too close— *The problem isn't with me, it's with him!*

The good news is that, in Christ, pruning, trimming back is preparation for powerful new growth. Yes, it can be painful—but, though change is not easy, it is freeing.

When we allow ourselves to let the crossroads change us—when we allow change not only to come *to* us, but *in* us—some spectacular things happen. Out-of-order priorities are re-ordered. Vision is clarified. Perspective broadens. If we are open to inner change. Even times of waiting can be refreshing, if we're open. We can refocus and redirect our attention when we open our hearts for needed change.

Not only that, hope is restored. Many times a crossroads experience proves to be just what we need to show us our need for renewed commitment—to a spouse, to God's service, and to spiritual growth.

For me (Neva) personally, I have discovered that if I simply open myself to God, even to unwanted change and to unknown possibilities, the times of the greatest change and challenge help me discover a heart-song of joy and gladness.

Seemingly impassable crossroads offer a rare opportunity to discover a reestablished or deeper exploration of our relationship with God. When we have to wait for answers to prayer—and stay open to the change that waiting can bring—some of us have discovered our faith is strengthened in a way that wouldn't have happened otherwise.

When we are open *to* change while we are having to make

*a* change, we can discover spiritual bondage being broken. A totally new freedom is born within us.

The list goes on and on. Joy is most often found within those who are open to change. Ministry opportunities, new purpose, and a change of direction come to those who choose to be open to change. We can rediscover dreams that were dying, or long ago dead, resurrected with new excitement and promise. And, of course, if we are ever to redefine our goals into reachable possibilities, it will be because we have chosen to be open to inner change.

## Change Point

Can you now identify an emotion that blocks you from making an important decision—such as *insecurity*, *fear*, or *doubt*? Could it be that this crossroads presents more than the need for a decision, but points out your need for a loving touch from God?

How do you face and manage the particular events or circumstances that force you to confront selfish and narrow attitudes or that challenge your personal prejudices? Could the Lord be opening some of your excess baggage and whispering into your heart, *Come on—let it go*?

How do you react when faced with past failures or disappointments? Crossroads situations often let those unresolved issues and unhealed hurts surface. Healing means change. Healing means freedom. It means forgiveness and wholeness. However, the challenge comes because for all the wonderful hope healing and wholeness promises, it also means responsibility.

I (Neva) once spoke to a group of church women, and at the end of the meeting a woman in a wheelchair approached me. She had been challenged by the words from John 5:5–6 "One who was there had been an invalid for thirty-eight years. When Jesus saw him lying there and learned that he had been in this condition for a long time, He asked him, 'Do you want to get well?' " For the first time the woman who approached me had heard the words of Christ echoing throughout her whole inner being. For years her family and friends had taken her to countless specialists. They took her to large meetings of well-known healing ministries. At the end of my meeting this day, she asked to be left alone with me.

"I've made an effort to get healed," she said through tears, "because when you're paralyzed it's what you *should* do." She blew her nose, then continued, "But, no one ever asked me the question 'Do you want to get well?' before. Everyone, including myself, assumed I wanted to be healed." She looked at her hands, the almost useless fingers. "I was injured in a fall from a horse when I was fourteen, my neck was broken and I have been mostly paralyzed since then.

"But, before that," she went on, "I was virtually unnoticed. I came from a large family. I am fourth from the eldest and third from the youngest. After the accident I was the family project. Everyone had to help. I had no use of my hands at first, and every movement was praised by the whole family. I was the center of attention. I was certain I would never walk again but it didn't matter. I was happy. If I had been healed, life would have resumed as usual, and I would again disappear within the family. Oh, people would probably talk about the accident, and they'd exclaim about the miracle healing but they might ignore *me*.

"So you see, it wasn't so bad. I met my husband when I was seventeen. His first wife had run off with another man. He laughed and said he was certain I would never do that. We were married when I turned nineteen."

She paused for a moment and caught her breath before she thoughtfully continued. "I have three children of my own now. I've never changed a diaper, never washed a tub of baby laundry. I've never had to drive, learn to cook, or do my own cleaning. Insurance and state benefits pick up all my medical expenses." She paused before admitting, "I really do like my life this way. I don't want to have to do the things others do. But today, I faced it, really for the first time—I don't want to change."

My message that day wasn't even about physical healing or wellness. It was about being serious and careful in our response when God speaks to the deeper issues of our lives. But, you see, this lady's problem, while appearing to be physical—was much deeper. Who knows, maybe she wouldn't have been healed even if her heart's desire *was* for healing. Unexplainably, many who seek and ask for healing are not healed. But she could have taken steps toward inner wholeness, no matter what her body was like. Sadly, she turned the wheelchair and slowly made her way back down the aisle of the church.

We *can* be changed but not as long as we're closed and resistant to change because we are protecting the life we've carefully arranged around ourselves. Sometimes risk and change itself is the step. Stepping into the unknown. Making a change when we cannot control all the issues and details. Will you have the courage to discover the power of positive change, available through the healing power of Christ? Will you let go of your control over circumstances and allow Him to be Lord of your life?

Often, an important detail of the man's story in John 5 is overlooked. Jesus didn't say "Get up and run tell your family," or "Send someone to get your friends so they can see you get healed." Jesus gave him a strange command when you think about it: "Get up! Pick up your mat and walk." At once the man was cured; he picked up his mat and walked.

Why is it strange? Jesus didn't give him even a moment to make the transition, to adjust to the difference between being sick and being well before he gave him the responsibility to pick up after himself. In fact, *his healing came with responsibility*. He changed from someone who *was* a responsibility to others into a person *of* responsibility.

That's change!

Standing alone in the quietness of the small church sanctuary watching the woman in the wheelchair leave, the Lord seemed to speak into my own heart. *You do the same thing. You go about the business of appearing to be in the right place. You pray the right prayers—but the issue is something entirely different. And often it concerns a need you won't admit or a change you refuse to make. Furthermore, it usually centers around a responsibility you are unwilling to take.*

Could this be so? I remember feeling no judgment for the woman, nor did I question God about why He didn't raise her from that wheelchair. You see, I too am a middle child of a large family. And, I too have had trauma or illness that I wanted to prolong just to get the attention it brought. Through repentance I had dealt with those issues long before. But I understood all too well the sad woman's inner need. But that afternoon I was presented with a personal challenge to change. Though I wasn't in a physical wheelchair, was I sitting in one *emotionally, spiritually*? How much responsibility had I gotten out of because I had been wounded, unappreciated, or neglected—or perceived myself to be?

How many bad attitudes had I harbored, begging for understanding and tolerance—rather than healing and strength?

Wholeness isn't being free from stress, anxiety, and pain. Wholeness is a bridge, it is what connects the tissue of our lives and personality to the lordship of Christ. Wholeness isn't the end—it's the means to becoming what God has designed us to become.

Jesus asks each of us the same question, do we really want to be well? It's a crossroads choice. And wholeness brings change. It's not only a step toward helping you deal with crossroads experiences, it is a step toward new responsibility. You too will become . . . to learn to take care of yourself, to find your identity and security in something, or rather *Someone* new.

Maybe you've reached this point before. Stepping into the stream you have carefully taken each step across the stones toward the other side. This chapter has helped you now see your need—and indeed, the opportunity—you have to change. You might even welcome it. We hope so, because a stepping-stone is no place to pitch a tent! Each stepping-stone leads to still another stepping-stone. Will you take this important step, will you accept new responsibility? Will you choose to become—to grow? Are you willing to let your crossroads change you? To become who and what God intended and, in fact, designed you to become all along?

As you can see, you've come to still another choice. No doubt about it—a most challenging choice. This is a pivotal decision. It's a choice on which the very direction of your life hinges. You can either go on or go back. For the moment you choose to be open to change and growth, accepting whatever responsibility being whole brings your way, you will be able to rise from your emotional wheelchair or pick up your mat and miraculously begin to walk as a healed person.

Then, without camping out on that new wonderful stepping-stone—will you stretch for the next?

# 13

# Becoming Responsible

---

## Choice #5

### Choose to accept responsibility.

---

Who could blame the man? Living poolside for thirty-eight years had denied him so many privileges. Certainly he had never traveled to distant cities or perhaps even crossed town. All he knew was the pool. The only ones he knew well were other poolside residents. That is, until the day Jesus came by, and he was challenged to pick up his bed instead of sitting all day on it. Of walking instead of lying. Of being involved, in contrast to being a spectator. Picking up his bed was the beginning of his new life of wholeness and responsibility.

But what if he was of our generation. Would he be expected to jump right in to responsibility? Who would blame the man for wanting to take a little time out to "regroup" or to "find himself"? Could he be criticized for wanting to do some exploring, to take some long-dreamed-of adventure or visit a distant place he had only heard of before?

Perhaps he would say, "I've been ill so long, I'll have to get used to being well before I can take a job." Or perhaps, "I just got rid of the burden—now you want to load me down with responsibility!"

The point is, there is much more to being well than just being healed. Becoming responsible is an essential key to maintaining healing and becoming whole. It's a package deal! Wholeness without responsibility is not wholeness at all.

Sadly, we live in a culture saturated with a *gimme* mentality. Tragically, the culture has not stopped with unbelievers, but has invaded the homes and churches of believers as well.

Do we really know what becoming responsible means? Do we know what is involved? Are we destined to define it in our own terms and determine for ourselves the challenge and call to become responsible? Unfortunately, our homes and churches are filled with irresponsible people.

## The Responsibility Taker

You know them—every club, circle, or committee has them. They are those who quickly rise to the top. They live as if they've been in charge since before the beginning. Making decisions is easy, so easy, in fact, they can take responsibility for anyone and everyone who cannot. Unfortunately, these people are answerable to no one, dependent on no one. The Responsibility Taker is known for getting things done—no matter what. There is no difference between their opinion and absolute truth—no other way but their way will do.

Responsibility Takers are driven by accomplishments and goals. Any plan other than theirs is unthinkable and destined for certain failure. Perfectionistic and narrow, the Responsibility Taker makes legalism into a fine art. These church heroes can peddle their power in a constant search for mighty exploits and super-human projects to perform. Driven people, often overworked, they can sometimes be seen coughing and sputtering miserably along the way as they overheat and burn up their emotional and spiritual engines. Responsibility Takers take responsibility beyond what is asked or even needed of them and aren't ashamed to talk about it. They conveniently ignore what the Bible says. "For everything in the world—the cravings of sinful man, the lust of his eyes and the boasting of what he has and does—comes not from the Father but from the world.''[1]

When confronted with a crossroads decision, Responsibility Takers plow right through, goals in sight and obstacles ignored. Unfortunately, they know from previous experience the meaning of the saying, "Not enough time to do it right, but plenty of time to do it over."

And what happens when they have taken on too much? When the responsibility they have taken on overwhelms them and wears them out? Often there's a Responsibility Assumer standing close-by to help out.

## The Responsibility Assumer

Those who stand by ready to receive what the Responsibility Taker can no longer handle are known as Responsibility Assumers. "I might as well assume this responsibility, it's always dumped in my lap sooner or later anyway." This guilt-driven person lives in the shadow of looming defeat.

These people base their life and acceptance on performance. Though tired of trying to measure up to *self-set, unreal* expectations and unreachable goals, they don't know how to live any differently.

What's more, the Responsibility Assumer is usually lonely. They cannot imagine life harnessed in a team, pulling the weight of life's load together. The Responsibility Assumer is not just unequally yoked—but usually solo-yoked. The Responsibility Assumer's conversation is a dead giveaway punctuated with "I should have's" and "I never should have's." They would love to know promises like this in experience: "This then is how we know that we belong to the truth, and how we set our hearts at rest in His presence whenever our hearts condemn us. For God is greater than our hearts, and He knows everything. Dear friends, if our hearts do not condemn us, we have confidence before God and receive from Him anything we ask, because we obey His commands and do what pleases Him."[2] But they suspect that such rest and peace is meant only for someone else.

Decisions come hard for the Responsibility Assumer and

---

[1] 1 John 2:16
[2] 1 John 3:19–22

crossroads are often defined as a crisis in the making. With no room for error, or grace to recover from mistakes, they freeze. Assuming all the while that if the decision goes sour, "It will be my fault." Afraid they might be unhappy, or that someone else will be, they delay many decisions until the decision makes itself—or wait until it's too late to decide, which is really the same.

When the Responsibility Assumer hears the Lord speaking about a personal or spiritual issue, they check out on God. Why? Because it's hard to depend on God when you believe God is depending on you. So, when met with personal failure the Responsibility Assumer pulls himself up by his bootstraps and vows to never let it happen again—to try harder than ever next time.

The Responsibility Assumer spends his prayer time repenting because the world hasn't been won to Christ already. And confessing how selfish and guilty he feels in *only* teaching a Sunday school class of small children when entire nations need evangelizing. This person reads John 3:16 and says, "Oh no! Jesus came because of me—it's my fault—I'm to blame!"

Each of us tend toward one end of the responsibility continuum or the other. However, we can leave our extreme position and *become responsible*.

Becoming responsible is not the same as taking responsibility, nor is it assuming responsibility. Becoming responsible has to do with what we *are* more than what we *do*. Becoming responsible is the goal of those whose hearts are totally committed to Christ. It is the development of the depth of character that reads John 3:16 and says, "God loved me so much, and knew I was helpless to do anything about my sinful state so He sent Christ, His only Son to do for me what I could not do for myself. He did what I needed, now I will do what He says." Becoming responsible is learning the joy of becoming a Responsibility Accepter.

## The Responsibility Accepter

Standing in stark contrast to both the Taker and the Assumer, the Responsibility Accepter is that person who stands, lives, and works in a healthy response to God and the lordship of Jesus Christ. Living under both the shadow of His wings and the orders of the Almighty, they know and appreciate the fact that they are not their own, that they've been bought with a price.[3] Tireless, faithful, grace-led believers who rest in knowing that God will enable every task He assigns and support every ministry He has called. Responsibility Accepters learn what it is to be trustworthy, confidential, and consistent.

Responsibility Accepters make decisions carefully, considering each option and weighing the consequences. They listen to advice, do their homework, and prepare themselves through prayers of submission and praise to God. Then prayerfully, trustfully, they step out in faith and make a choice.

And if it all goes sour? The Responsibility Taker discounts the consequences, saying, "Well, I did the best I could. Get someone else to do it next time—I have taken on a new responsibility.," The Assumer says, "I knew it. I can't do anything right. It won't happen next time—because there won't be a next time!" But the Responsibility Accepter says, "Maybe I should try that again. Let's see if there is a different way to approach this decision. What is God saying to me through this experience?"

Jesus knew all three types of people among his disciples. "I'll do it," is a statement most of us would expect of Peter. But in John 6, we see Philip assuming Jesus was giving him a responsibility and assuming there was no other way to feed the several thousands of people gathered there on the hillside than to go to the nearest store for food.

Yet the story doesn't end there. Andrew was the one who spoke up and became a Responsibility Accepter. Looking around he found a boy's lunch—a few small barley rolls and a couple of sardines. Not much—but hey, what else have we got? You see, Responsibility Accepters have learned that you accept responsibility for what you *have*, and give it *all*—even if you know it's not enough to begin with. Philip looked at the people, Andrew looked at the Provider. Philip saw the need, Andrew saw Jesus. Philip backed away, Andrew stepped forward. Philip saw the problem, Andrew saw a possibility.

And where was Peter, the Responsibility Taker? If he was like most Responsibility Takers he wasn't about to get mixed

---

[3] 1 Corinthians 6:20

up in this situation. Takers want only to get involved when success is all but guaranteed.

## Becoming

*Becoming responsible* is possible, even for Responsibility Takers and Assumers. It's part of the growing Christian's life and destiny. Being a Responsibility Accepter may be an easier task for some than for others—but it's not a characteristic we're born with. It's what we become as we mature. It's something we come to be, to change into. It happens when we choose to change in our crossroads experiences and it can be described as becoming a disciple—not just a Christian. And it can happen to you.

Becoming a disciple is not something you can take into your own hands, nor is it a burden God is waiting to sling across your already drooping shoulders. It's not something He's been waiting to dump into your lap. It's an offer. It's an opportunity. You cannot assume this responsibility, nor can you take it—you must accept it.

If you return to our stream-crossing analogy, it is only fair to warn you that this is the last stepping-stone you can use to turn back. In a sense, becoming a disciple is the point of no return. But really, you've come so far, would you honestly consider going back now when you've already crossed the halfway point?

The best is about to be. . . .

# 14

# Going for the Gold

---

**Choice #6**

**Choose to become a disciple, in order to
grow as a Christian.**

---

Hundreds of thousands gathered recently in a small town in Norway. The survivors of a brutal civil war in their homeland were there, as well as Lyubov, the ballerina-turned-skier from Russia, and the first American bobsled team to pilot an American-made bobsled—all converging with other world-class athletes for sixteen incomparable days and nights of athletic competition. They met beneath the blazing Olympic torch to compete on the sub-zero slopes, to challenge each other on the ice in the Viking ship speed-skating arena, and to relax around the gigantic carved wooden troll in a local restaurant. Years of hard work, personal sacrifice, and intense training culminated on these historical days for one common goal—*to go for the gold*.

Watching from an armchair by the fire, many stay-at-home fans and admirers watched skiers slice through freezing wind, skaters cut deep scars with champion precision in the ice, and the daring lugers plunged toward the finish line. People everywhere were caught up watching the rugged athletes push the limits, take unbelievable chances to lay it all on the line as they broke old and set new records of skill, speed, and endurance. Many wept with joy for those who, in less than a blink of an eyelash, exhibited the skill and confidence necessary to make split-second decisions that won them hairsbreadth victories. Some cried with sorrow for those who took shattering falls, or made a *hundredth-of-a-second* mistake that changed their lives forever.

Guts and glory—it's a trait admired by those who watched. But there is more to the Olympic Games than gold, silver, or bronze medals. Ask the coaches, the families, and the athletes themselves.

For example, ask the bobsledders who spend twenty-four hundred percent more time honing the blades on their sleds than they do on the course—four hours of perfecting, sanding, and polishing for every *fifty-two-second* run. The most tedious task of the bobsledder is not successfully executing the make-or-break start, nor is it navigating the dangerous turns. It isn't the long straightaway toward the finish line—it is the runners, sharpened before each and every race.

Or you could ask the figure skaters. Listening to music to find just the right piece for their four-minute free program can take months. Exercise, ballet, and fitness training go on relentlessly. Difficult jumps are made literally thousands of times in practice. Fifteen to twenty years of unending practices take place behind closed doors or in lonely studios, seen only by their coaches, before they finally earn the right to skate in the Olympics.

Ask the skiers about the never-ending training, competing, retraining, and more competition. Summer and winter their physically demanding sport requires personal determination, untold sacrifice, and a level of hard work and commitment most of us know nothing about, for a vision we can't begin to understand.

But the most intriguing part of it all is the inspiration they bring to the entire watching world. Who didn't find motivation to discover a new perspective or sense an inner urge to keep trying in their own struggles when Dan Jansen won his first gold medal in his last possible attempt? Who didn't glory in the moment as Bonnie Blair became the most "medalled" woman in American Olympic history? And who didn't share inwardly the moment of victory with Gordeeva and Grinkov, the young pairs figure skaters from Russia standing together on the winner's podium?

We admire these outstanding accomplishments. We vicariously thrill at their achievements and mourn at their defeats. From our recliner-chair position, our eyes swell with tears as the winners stand on the highest podium, hearing their national anthem and watching their flag being hoisted high above the crowd of cheering spectators. It is a thrill very few ever experience firsthand.

Perhaps we thrill with them more because of the stories *behind* the success rather than in the actual gold-medal moment. The events that shaped their lives, the dedication of the coaches, and the total commitment of the athletes themselves interests us, because they speak to our own struggles and obstacles. And well they should. The stories behind the athletes are stirring accounts of obstacles overcome and immovable barriers conquered through total dedication and intense discipline.

Perhaps we sit riveted to the Olympic broadcasts because, in our own way, in our own circumstance, we too are *going for the gold.*

Our events may not attract media coverage and national attention, but our victories are just as significant. The stories behind our achievements and accomplishments may never be told, but they are just as inspiring and motivating. Our obstacles are just as overwhelming and our barriers just as interminable as any gold medalist ever encountered.

What's more, we are made of the same champion material as any wearer of an Olympic gold medal. It takes the same determination, sacrifice, and personal commitment to live and walk as a champion through everyday life as it does to soar down a ski slope and fly through the winter sky to land a record-breaking jump.

We identify with them because we, too, have made a determined decision. We have chosen to be content only when we have reached for the gold. Sound impossible? Until we take one very important step of choice, it probably is.

It is only when you and I decide to become more than average, make the commitment to become more than we have been perceived to be and determine no matter what the cost we will meet one important goal: To accept the responsibility to change and grow from a Christian into a disciple.

And when we do, the training moves to a level known only to world-class, winning athletes.

Drilling, training, and exercise is the way of life for an Olympic champion and they, too, must become a regular part of our routine. Not in the same physical sense, but as we watch the best athletes in the world compete and thrill at their victories, let us learn from their rigorous training schedules as well.

## Training for Gold

*A medalist begins training as early as possible.* Stories of skaters and skiers beginning in their sport almost before they could walk are not that unusual. Is it the same for Christians? "Let them alone," some say about new Christians, "they will run into hard times soon enough. Let them enjoy being a Christian awhile before they have to learn about warfare and faith." How true—and how sad that we aren't training them early for the hard times we know will come!

*A medalist trains all the muscles of his body—not just a few.* Is that true of the church? Do we train all the parts of the body of Christ to work in harmony to work as one for one goal and cause? Do we train ourselves individually to be balanced or do we prefer to specialize on certain ideas or doctrines? For example, do we practice prayer *and* fasting? Do we tend toward extremes and routines in our private worship? Can we only witness with a pamphlet in hand and not at all without one? In other words, do we *cross-train* as disciples in training?

*A medalist learns the fundamentals of his sport before ever entering a competition.* The skiers Tommy Moe and Pekabo Street learned to successfully navigate the bunny hill before they hit the big slopes. Disciples in training take the time to learn the basics well and then to teach others those same fundamentals.

*A medalist knows his equipment.* The Olympic Games is not the best time to try out a new sled, wear new skates, or experiment with new skis. Disciples know this principle well. If we are to carry out our commission with champion endurance and medalist quality we must be very well acquainted with our equipment. The Word of God is a sword we must get used to wielding. Faith is best exercised and kept as sharp as a bobsledder's runners. Hours and hours of preparation, strategy, and training for a few seconds in any given situation is not the most inviting prospect—but do we dare to face life-changing decisions any other way?

*A medalist enters many smaller events before finally going for the gold.* Each competition is training for the next. Even losses are stepping-stones toward that long-awaited moment on the winner's podium. Champions use each experience and event—even their crossroads events—as learning places. Each victory or failure has training value for the upcoming events and crossroads still ahead.

*A medalist learns from his mistakes.* A fall doesn't have to be fatal. Ski jumpers relax as soon as they realize they've lost control. Skaters learn to go with the stumble instead of fighting against it. Later, they examine video footage of their performances, seek advice, and put themselves under a professional coach. Disciples in training find mentors and practice their faith under the watchful eye of a "coach," while they make smaller decisions, accept smaller responsibilities, learn from their mistakes, and build on their successes.

*A medalist learns the importance of rest.* No matter how fit, how fine-tuned, and how skilled an athlete is, lack of rest can jangle his nerves, corrupt his judgment, and affect his endurance. Athletes take a day off now and then, listen to soothing music, see the sights, and spend time reading or with friends, away from their sport. Disciples must do the same. Day and night, one phone call after another, pressures at work and at home—we need to build in breaks from such intensity. When you need to perform at your best, lack of rest can send you sliding into a nearby barrier, like a fallen skier catapulting toward a snowbank.

*A champion knows how to focus.* Distractions and pressures must submit to concentration on the course or routine just ahead. Even the gold medal must be forgotten for the moment as the athlete accepts the responsibility to perform what was accomplished in practices many times before.

We've so much important training to do. Disciples train themselves to know how to hold on when others will let go. They know how to continue when others quit, and how to believe when others doubt. Disciples learn to maintain joy in the face of sorrow, to confront fear with courage, to challenge themselves with openness and vulnerability when every instinct screams for protection and privacy. Disciples learn to say *no* to the unbelieving voices inside in order to say *yes* to freshness and strength that comes from following only God's voice.

In all the interviews in Lillehammer, Norway, not one athlete said they were there by accident. Every single gold medalist had targeted his life with complete focus toward that milestone moment. Not one athlete was unaware of the significance of the games, the records, and the medals. Many were there solely to take first place in their area of competition. Others knew they were only preparing for the gold in the competition four years away. It is the same with disciples. Discipleship is not something that happens by accident. Nor is it something achieved by osmosis or assumption. Discipleship doesn't happen simply because you dream about it—but because you follow that dream with and through disciplined training.

Disciples live with purpose. They strive for excellence in their marriage and families. They work at being a good friend and make the effort necessary to build strong, healthy friendships.

Disciples are people who search out and discover their place of ministry within the body of Christ. They choose to look beyond their own needs and explore instead their gifts. Their entire motivation changes from getting to giving, and personal satisfaction takes a backseat to service.

Disciples are people of resolution—who have made up their minds. They have settled it once and for all. They set their hearts and sights on what could be . . . instead of dwelling on what was or what should have been.

How about you? Would you like to be able to curb your appetites, control your tongue, and ride herd on runaway attitudes? Does a life free from indirection and confusion interest you? Do you long to be a person who approaches crossroads and the many challenging choices they present with courage and wisdom?

Then the life of a disciple-in-training beckons. It will take discipline to become a disciple. You will learn that your time will be just as involved as your heart. Your money will be affected as will your habits and hobbies. The disciple learns to manage his or her own faith, just as the figure skater must take his own spins and leaps. The Holy Spirit will come alongside and stick as closely as any coach working with his athlete. Your whole world will become focused and even some things you once found essential will seem trivial and unimportant.

The life of a disciple is not dull, nor is it drudgery. The life of a disciple is an *adventure*, full of exploration and discovery!

Discipleship is a training camp filled with other disciples in training, learning to run alongside each other—completing, not competing. It is a way of life filled with visionaries, mentors, and supporters. It is charged with love and steadied by accountability.

Disciples keep eternity in sharp focus. We are immortal beings, mortal only as far as this world is concerned. We train our hearts and sharpen our minds as much as the bobsledder labors over the runners of his sled. We pay as much attention to wearing the armor of God as the skier selects equipment, gear, and technique. We concern ourselves with overcoming doubt and prepare ourselves for spiritual warfare, just as an athlete would in competition. And we train by choosing to accept the responsibility of becoming—the responsibility to change.

We begin by accepting a different view of ourselves. To accept ourselves as winners, not losers. As people infused with the energy of God's Spirit pulsating within our inner selves. To see ourselves as responsible people of great possibility and potential for being world-changers not just record-breakers. We accept the fact that we are disciples in training. We base our identity and our worth in what Christ has done for and in us. We find new security, hope, and faith—not in our skill or talent as the physical athlete does—but in Jesus Christ, our Redeemer.

And, if that weren't enough, just like Tommy Moe, Bonnie Blair, Dan Jansen, Torvill and Dean, and the Russian ballerina who won the gold in seven Olympic cross-country events—we, too, will be known forever as *champions*.

Furthermore, we're out there every day in the center of the arena, giving it all we've got in the event every single person enters—life.

When it's over? The Olympic winner's ceremony pales in comparison. Can you even imagine the unfurling banner of our Lord Jesus Christ being raised, millions of cheering voices joining together to sing "All Hail the Power of Jesus' Name" while angels circle gloriously overhead? Picture yourself standing on the winner's podium as the Prince of Peace himself rises from His place of honor beside the Father, majestic trumpets blaring as He descends the steps of the throne. Can you imagine the hush that spreads over the vast host of witnesses as the Lamb of God steps toward you, coming to place, not a lowly gold medal hanging on a ribbon around your neck, but a glorious crown upon your head? Just imagine the deafening cheers as the King of Glory pulls you close to His breast in a loving embrace before He takes your hand and leads you to be presented before the Father—our matchless Father!

If we are ever to make it as a disciple, the picture just described will have to be forever emblazoned within our minds and branded on our hearts. A picture of the triumph and victory of Calvary must be held high in the moments of decision, and gloriously overshadow us as we make our crossroads choices and navigate our difficult and trying circumstances.

Come on, Disciple-Champion! Get into training! Go for the gold!

# 15

# Choosing Commitment

---

## Choice #7

### Choose to become a person of lasting and solid commitment.

---

Ann is a gold-medalist disciple. Her story is that of a real disciple who stumbled, got up, and learned how to keep placing every experience under the lordship of Christ. She was a truly successful crossroads navigator.

As a young woman, she married a Christian man, but after she became pregnant he walked out on her. Two months later, a doctor convinced her she needed a complete hysterectomy or she would die. She allowed him to take the life of her preborn child, rendering her sterile in the process—only to find out the doctor was a charlatan. Dreams of a husband and family were wiped out.

Ann fought off the urge to pull into herself. Believing that Christ could use the love she would have given to her own family, she eventually accepted a position as a house-mother in a ministry for troubled young women. As these girls found love and direction from Ann, she became for many of them the mother they'd never had. As they left the home and went on to marry, she became "Aunt Ann" to their babies. And yet. . . .

After a time, Ann became an assistant to a wealthy Christian executive. Through the years she grew to be a personal friend of the man's whole family—a confidante of the man's wife. A trusted friend.

After twenty years, the executive's wife succumbed to cancer. In his grief, the man turned to Ann. It seemed so natural, so God-ordered. By now, Ann was in her 50s. Maybe God had finally brought the answer to her emotional, spiritual, and financial needs. Her heart was opening fast.

Then one day the man confessed, "Ann, I'm sorry. I was confused. I don't really love you . . . not in the way it would take for us to be married. Please forgive me."

In her devastation, Ann said she forgave him. But inwardly the battle began. Would she ever escape the feeling that she had been *used*? Bitterness and rage began to eat at her day and night.

In the midst of her pain and despair, Ann cried out to God. In all those years, no viable opportunity to re-marry had ever presented itself. This seemed so cruel. *I don't want to end my days as a bitter, lonely old woman. All I've ever wanted was a family of my own . . . and I can't see how it will ever happen. I'll be 60 before long.*

Now she was looking for a new job, as well. A friend at church told her about a doctor, Don Smith (not his real name), who was looking for a live-in companion for his wife, Maria— a victim of debilitative cancer.

Ann resisted. It sounded like a repeat of the past. *One more chance to be used . . . until I'm used up,* she told herself.

As she prayed about her need for a job, the doctor's wife kept coming to mind, no matter how much she resisted. *I'm not willing to go through this all over again,* she told God.

But she was at a crossroads. The only job on the horizon was this one. And it seemed as if a voice inside was telling her, *You set yourself aside for My use when you became my follower and disciple. You can let Me choose your way, or go your own way.*

Ann is one of those rare and wonderful people who—even when it is desperately hard—refuses to let herself be defined by her past. *I will open myself to you, Father. If this woman needs me, and if this is your provision for me . . . I'll go. I know that you know what's best for me. And Lord, I'll trust you to help me with my need for love and companionship.*

For nearly three years, Ann was best friend and nursemaid to Maria. Once again, Ann found herself drawn into the center of a family—accepting it as a substitute family, because she had none of her own. What began as a job, grew into a deep friendship. So much so that as Maria came within weeks of her death, she summoned Ann to her bedside and stunned her with a request.

"I love you, Ann," Maria said, squeezing her hand.

"I love you, too" said Ann. She felt as if her heart was breaking.

"Don and I have been talking about what he'll do after I'm gone. You may think this is a shocking thing for me to say— but I can't think of a finer person to leave behind with my husband than you."

Maria paused, and Ann stared into her friend's eyes. What was she saying. "Oh, Maria . . . I . . . Don . . ." she fumbled for words.

"You know me well enough to know I'm not a meddler," said Maria. "But the three of us have become so close. You're family, Ann." Maria shifted her position painfully. "Well, who knows," she said, changing her tone, "God can do anything. I just have a hunch. . . ."

In less than a month Maria was gone. Ann moved out of her room in Dr. Smith's home to avoid any awkwardness, but she did help the Smiths' grown children and the grandchildren to pray through and accept Maria's death.

No doubt you have seen the end of this story coming by now. Six months after Maria's death, Dr. Smith did come to see Ann and take her out to dinner. It was a gentle evening of friendly conversation, mostly centering on memories of Maria. Dr. Smith admitted that several nurses at the local hospital had zeroed-in on him within weeks of the funeral.

"But I can't find another woman who's really my type," he said, shaking his head, "that is, no one besides you, Ann."

He slid his hand across the table and covered hers with it. Here they were, two lonely people in their early 60s, with lifetimes of love and loss, pain and joy, brought together in a most unusual way.

Ann says that something slid into place in her heart in that moment. She knew beyond knowing that, because she had continued to follow Christ, He had always been working out His plan for her, guiding her through every crossroad even when she felt abandoned and bereft.

Today, too, Don and his children and grandchildren say they are sure Ann has been God's special provision—a treasure He saved to give them after their wife and mother's death.

"Ann has lost so much in her life—yet she learned how to trust Christ anyway when things didn't go well for her," says one of Don's sons. "She has such light shining in her. She was able to lead one of my daughters out of drugs and rebellion—just because Amy saw authentic Christianity in Ann.

"There are no words to say how grateful we are to have Ann tucked into the center of our family. Some people might have a hard time with this—but God gave us more than a companion for Dad. He gave us a new mother and grandmother."

Ann's story says a lot about life, discipleship, and the one ingredient most needed to make a champion. Ann had committed herself to Christ, and so she was willing to push on at His direction, even when that one dream in her heart was not realized for so long. She brought everything she had to her work for other people, when she could have pulled into herself because of so many disappointments. Instead, her life is now filled with love from the many people she has loved.

Trusting herself fully to God—even her unrealized dreams—Ann pressed on. And today, at last, she has her dream.

It can be so easy to sit back, admire—even be jealous of those who have found their dreams and reached their goals. It's tempting to believe that those who started with so little and have come so far have had some kind of advantage or a "lucky break."

Is there a difference between those who *dwell* in their dreams and those who *realize* their dreams? Is there a deciding factor between those who successfully navigate their crossroads experiences and those who don't?

In the previous chapter, we looked at the discipline needed for a medal-winning performance. But as you can see if you look at the life of someone like Ann, it takes commitment to follow Christ all the way to the goal—even if the goal seems to recede beyond your reach.

If discipline is behind a world-class performance, then

*commitment* is behind discipline. *Commitment is the decision we make to become attached to a choice, or course of action,* from which there is no turning back, no alternative. A sporting performance with discipline—but without commitment—would mean that your body might perform flawlessly, but your soul would be somewhere else. You see, performance based on discipline only, without commitment, may have technical perfection but would have no heart.

Unfortunately, knowing that commitment requires putting your heart into a decision, many hold back and resist commitment.

Commitment means we not only accept a responsibility, but feel it—a risk many are afraid to take. It's true, commitment holds potential for both increased joy and compounded sorrow. If we make a commitment and then fail, we not only lose what we were committed to but lose some of our self, as well.

Fortunately, there are very few things that require a once-and-for-all commitment. Very few commitments are really lifelong.

One of the commitments we *are* called to make permanent is our relationship with Christ. Being fully committed to Christ is not an option if we are to become successful at navigating life's crossroads. We tend to want safety nets and rescue teams standing by should our relationship with Jesus take us through rough waters or lonely places. We want options clearly defined and readily available should our choice to serve Christ threaten our personal ambitions.

Becoming wholly committed to Christ is choosing to travel with a one-way ticket. This is especially difficult in our materialistic society, where it is unthinkable to give your life and heart totally to much of anything other than personal goals and desires. Yet people seek recreational activities and death-defying thrills that require such commitment.

For example, after carefully going through the necessary training, the sky diver finally climbs aboard a small plane. Following a thorough check of his equipment, reaching the right altitude, and flying above the desired location, all his options are left behind the moment he jumps free of the aircraft. Once he's out the door, he's headed toward the ground—totally committed to the jump.

Airline passengers know what it is to feel the aircraft leave the ground, and from that moment on be committed to go where the plane goes—hopefully to the destination printed on their ticket.

## Levels of Commitment

To become a person of commitment it would be helpful to understand the several levels, or phases, we go through before our commitment becomes permanent. To misunderstand this can set us up for failure time and time again, leave us gun-shy and afraid of making lasting choices or binding decisions.

1. *Commitment's Casual Level—Attraction*

"Some enchanted evening, you will see a stranger, across a crowded room. . . ." So goes the romantic tune from the past. Fascination, even interpreted as love at first sight, is not the same as lifelong commitment. Awareness of someone interesting doesn't always develop into the romance of the ages. Nor does a date or two mean a wedding will happen soon. Not unless the relationship moves to and then through the next levels.

2. *Commitment's Exclusive Level—Courtship*

"I only have eyes for you. . . ." is the theme song of this level of commitment. In the '50s and '60s, young people called it going steady. In the '90s it's going out. Totally focused on each other, fascination turns to love. Couples listen to each other breathe on the phone and look deep into each other's eyes when together. Dating others is out of the question at this level of commitment, even though it hasn't reached permanency yet and won't for some time.

3. *Commitment's Trial Level—Engagement*

Eventually, if all goes like a romance novel, the "question" is popped and the couple is rapturously happy as they announce their engagement. "I love you," he says, "and I can't imagine life without you. Let's run away and get married." But, if the commitment is to fully mature, hastily running away to begin a permanent commitment is a mistake without fully experiencing the trial level.

"I love you and can't imagine my life without you. *But*—I believe our marriage to be so important that I am in favor of finding ways to secure our relationship before we enter the adjustments marriage will require." Very few probably make that statement, but this level of relational development is essential for successful marriage. It is the time to seek counsel, as a shift occurs from focusing on each other to exploring the relationship. This is essential preparation for the final and permanent level of commitment, marriage.

4. *Commitment's Permanence—Marriage*

Finally the day arrives, the wedding chapel is filled with flowers and happy guests. The nervous groom claims his lovely bride in front of family and friends. Together, bathed in candlelight, they make their pledges promising to stay in the relationship and to work through life's problems together. Two separate lives through each prior level of commitment unite at this level. At previous levels of commitment, either party could have walked away, but from now on—neither will without paying a heavy emotional price and causing heavy emotional damage to the other.

Courtship and marriage, while an easily understood illustration of commitment, is not the only commitment that moves through each level. All commitments do to one degree or another, even our relationship with Christ.

Ephesians 5:28–32 contains these words:

"In this same way, husbands ought to love their wives as their own bodies. He who loves his wife loves himself. After all, no one ever hated his own body, but he feeds and cares for it, just as Christ does the church—for we are members of His body. For this reason a man will leave his father and mother and be united to his wife, and the two will become one flesh. This is a profound mystery—but I am talking about Christ and the church."

Listen to the words taken from a traditional Christian wedding ceremony and see how they speak to us of our relationship to Christ:

" . . . in the presence of this company . . ."

Matthew 10:32: "Whoever acknowledges me before men, I will also acknowledge him before my Father in heaven."

While the details of our relationship are personal and many times quite private, the relationship is anything but secret.

" . . . love, honor and obey . . ."

1 Kings 8:61: "But your hearts must be fully committed to the LORD our God, to live by His decrees and obey His commands, as at this time."

Love is something we do, not just something we feel.

" . . . through sunshine and shadow . . ."

Psalm 37:3–6: "Trust in the LORD and do good; dwell in the land and enjoy safe pasture. Delight yourself in the LORD and He will give you the desires of your heart. Commit your way to the LORD; trust in Him and He will do this: He will make your righteousness shine like the dawn, the justice of your cause like the noonday sun."

Day in and day out, season upon season, our relationship with Christ becomes the basis for our lifestyle, meaning, and purpose.

" . . . a covenant of promise . . ."

Ephesians 2:12–13: "Remember that at that time you were separate from Christ, excluded from citizenship in Israel and foreigners to the covenants of the promise, without hope and without God in the world. But now in Christ Jesus you who once were far away have been brought near through the blood of Christ."

His covenant is already fulfilled, my only promise I can make to Him is to rely on that covenant, to depend on His grace.

" . . . forsaking all others . . ."

Exodus 20:2–6 "I am the LORD your God, who brought you out of Egypt, out of the land of slavery. You shall have no other gods before me. You shall not make for yourself an idol in the form of anything in heaven above or on the earth beneath or in the waters below. You shall not bow down to them or worship them; for I, the LORD your God, am a jealous God, punishing the children for the sins of the fathers to the third and fourth generation of those who hate me, but showing love to a thousand generations of those who love me and keep my commandments."

Philippians 1:21: "For to me, to live is Christ and to die is gain."

Matthew 10:37–39: "Anyone who loves his father or mother more than me is not worthy of me; and anyone who loves his son or daughter more than me is not worthy of me; and anyone who does not take his cross and follow me is not worthy of me. Whoever finds his life will lose it, and whoever loses his life for my sake will find it."

Mark 10:21: "Jesus looked at him and loved him. 'One thing you lack,' He said. 'Go, sell everything you have and give

108 / *Living By Chance or By Choice*

to the poor, and you will have treasure in heaven. Then come, follow me.' "

Idols fall in the context of our loving relationship with our living God. Our dreams and ambitions lie silent and submissive before His mighty love. His jealousy guards us, His love sustains us and His ways are made clear to us. His life is now our life. No person, no thing, and no other way will do.

" . . . a promise of faithfulness . . ."

Joshua 1:5: "No one will be able to stand up against you all the days of your life. As I was with Moses, so I will be with you; I will never leave you nor forsake you."

Our security is in His ability to perform, not ours. His faithfulness is demonstrated throughout history and before. He knows what never and forever means.

" . . . in plenty and want, in joy and sorrow, in sickness and health . . ."

Psalms 23:1–6 "The LORD is my shepherd, I shall not be in want. He makes me lie down in green pastures, He leads me beside quiet waters, He restores my soul. He guides me in paths of righteousness for His name's sake. Even though I walk through the valley of the shadow of death, I will fear no evil, for you are with me; your rod and your staff, they comfort me. You prepare a table before me in the presence of my enemies. You anoint my head with oil; my cup overflows. Surely goodness and love will follow me all the days of my life, and I will dwell in the house of the LORD forever."

This is a relationship not dependent on or affected by changing circumstances, but based on the unchanging mercy and favor of God through them.

" . . . as long as we both shall live . . ."

John 3:16: "For God so loved the world that He gave His one and only Son, that whoever believes in Him shall not perish but have eternal life."

Because we have made Him our choice, we begin to understand the seriousness of making other commitments. We no longer make them hurriedly or take them lightly. We become people of our word, choosing to do what we say we will do and choosing to carry responsibilities to full-term, because finishing commitments is an expression of our personal commitment to Christ.

It is by the strength of our commitment to Christ that we are sustained through hard times, the way Ann was sustained through all her difficulties. When we make this depth of commitment to Christ, it will carry over to all other commitments for one simple reason: We have chosen to go beyond making commitments to being a person of commitment.

A person who has made such choices comes to know both by experience and by faith the meaning of Jesus' words to His Father: "I have brought you glory on earth by completing the work you gave me to do."

A person of commitment also understands the words of the apostle Paul: "I have fought the good fight, I have finished the race, I have kept the faith."[1]

And finally, a person of commitment experiences the promise of 2 Chronicles 16:9: "For the eyes of the LORD range throughout the earth to strengthen those whose hearts are fully committed to Him."

Yes, commitment is a choice. A choice each of us must make if we are going to successfully navigate all of life's choices and changes.

A person of commitment knows that any crossroads experience or choice is presented within the context of a secure, solid permanent relationship with Jesus Christ. The days of going-it-alone are over. Submitted believers—those who are determined to be affectionately bonded in unity with Jesus Christ—find that many of the decisions others struggle with are already made in the light of their relationship with Christ.

When you are in a committed, personal relationship with Jesus Christ, you have a security that cannot be lost, a faith that cannot be shattered, and a hope that cannot dim. You become whole—your promises are unbroken, and your heart undivided. Not perfect, but *complete*. Abandoned to Him, you are consistently getting better and better. Because there is One who is committed to perfecting you!

---

[1] 2 Timothy 4:7

# 16

# Stop, Look, and Listen

---

### Choice #8

**Successful Crossroads navigators have
chosen to keep their spiritual eyes
and ears open.**

---

One of the telltale signs of middle age is the need for bi-
focal lenses. When the eyes tire easily and the drugstore-va-
riety reading glasses don't help much, you have to make an
appointment for an eye exam.

It's not only our physical vision that needs adjustment and
correction. Little by little, our spiritual vision can become
blurred by circumstances or distorted by disappointment or
personal struggle. We simply don't see things quite as clearly
as in the past. We seem to run into blank walls. We grow tired
while trying to make sense out of difficult circumstances. We
become weak wrestling with situations that get blown out of
proportion. Stumbling our way around, we are tempted to

once again assume the crash position and stay there indefinitely.

When that happens, it's time to stop, take a moment, and ask the Lord for a "vision check."

## Checking Your Vision

Sitting quietly before God for a few moments, ask Him to help you by giving you a vision check. We can hear Him speak to us from Proverbs 29:18: "Where there is no vision, the people perish." (KJV)

Corrected vision is behind the Peace Corps-type concept that says I can give you a whole bushel of corn and feed you for a while, but if I teach you to grow corn you can feed yourself and others. Missionaries have learned that concept and begin *training* converts immediately, so that indigenous churches last beyond the lifetime of the missionary.

We faced that choice in writing this book. We could have written a how-to book on making decisions. But life is made up of complexities, and a simple checklist will not answer your need for wisdom when you come to future crossroads. We have purposely chosen this approach, which is to help you see the choices you can make to become a successful decision-maker, rather than cleverly helping you to make a one-time decision. A periodic "vision check" is part of becoming a responsible decision-maker.

Physically, we depend on an optometrist or an ophthalmologist to check our eyesight—spiritually, we check in with God. He alone can determine the correction needed.

Remember when Jesus took the blind man to the edge of the village? After having spit on his eyes, the man reported seeing people as trees walking. Jesus touched his eyes again and *then* he saw everything clearly. People were no longer seen as trees, but as they really were.[1] Isn't that what we need when our spiritual vision has become blurred and focus is painfully impossible?

This vision correction is what will help you put the last several chapters into focus. It is what will give you a sense of receiving fresh guidance from the Lord.

If you want to see with corrected vision, you will set out

---

[1] Mark 8:22–25

with a determination to pursue an intimate walk with God. Make the effort to deepen your relationship with Him. Let Him make the corrections needed so you can focus clearly on Him. Seeking the Lord will correct your spiritual vision by helping you to objectively see and assess your strengths, weaknesses, and gifts. He will help you discover where your gifts can best be used, and how to make them available.

Let God give you a new hunger for Holy Spirit-empowered living. Let Him help you see your need for His divine involvement. Let Him bring the opportunity you need *to* you, and the service others need *through* you.

We've said all this in order that you might understand and be able see your crossroads choices clearly. But also, to see clearly through your crossroads—to catch a vision of what is beyond each crossroads.

This point is made so beautifully in the story of Sir Edmond Hillary, who led the first expedition to the top of the world's highest peak, Mount Everest. The wonder of the story isn't what happened at that historical destination, but that climbing to the highest peak in the world led him to a whole new beginning. Life didn't end at the summit for Hillary, it took an unexpected dramatic turn there. High above a little village in Nepal, Hillary put his footprint on a mountain peak no one else had ever climbed. But down below, at the foot of the mountain, he put his imprint on people no one else had ever heard of. After his ascent to the formidable mountain peak in the Himalayas, he came back to the villages at the base. There at the foot of the mountain he made his greatest, though quietest, contribution. In these humble, remote villages he saw the danger of a unique people becoming extinct due to a lack of orientation to the outside world, medical care, and education.

Schools were soon built and teachers imported. Willing and inquisitive minds gladly opened to an entire world through books. Hospitals and medical personnel came soon after. Sir Edmond Hillary became a folk hero. Ask the young mother from Nepal if reaching the top of Mount Everest was as important as saving the life of her baby. Ask the village chief if his historic expedition was as impressive as learning to read alongside the children.

Sir Edmond Hillary did much more than take the first expedition to the top of an untouched mountain. He made more than history—he made a difference. He not only reached the mountain peak with his team, but he brought the world to the villagers. More important than discovering a route to the summit, he discovered that changing someone else's life can change your own.

Successful crossroads navigators discover the same truth. They discover that no matter how high the personal achievement, making a difference in the valleys is what matters most. That discovery can only come if our spiritual vision is corrected enough to see life's true need—only if we can see for ourselves the difference that waits to be made and how we can be the ones to make it.

How about it? When is your next appointment for a vision checkup?

The next section of this book is written to help you build deeper spiritual foundations in your life. It isn't meant to be a quick read, but a series of decisions you think through carefully, because they will fundamentally alter all the decisions you make from now on. For those of you who need to make a decision rather quickly, we recommend that you turn to Section Four through the end. But remember to come back to Section Three in a more relaxed time. It *will* change your life!

# Part Three

## Sucessful Crossroads Navigators Learn to Become People of Purpose

Having certain issues settled is basic to a stable, growing character. Decisions will always need to be made, yet we can be at ease, as though a major part of our decision was already made.

Settled issues give us an edge—and it gives us purpose. Have you settled personal issues and, in the process, discovered *purpose*?

# 17

# Knowing God's Will

---

### Purpose #1

**Make it your purpose to discover and
explore God's will. Settle it once and for
all that God's will is not to be regarded
only as a momentary directional signal,
but an overall life-guide. It involves not
just your circumstances, but you.**

---

While it may seem like it, your crossroads experiences
have not caught God off-guard. Maybe you have been taken by
surprise but He has not. Your life may certainly *feel* out of control, but it is not out of control for Him. God does have a plan
for your life. And what's more, He will show it to you.

However, there may be well-meaning folk who give you a
wrong impression of what they perceive God's will to be. But
*God is behind your struggle—in fact, it's probably part of His
plan.*

It is not unusual to stand beside someone during a time of

confusing crisis or emergency and hear words like:

"I guess God has a purpose in all of this."

"Don't question. God is in control. He knows what's best."

"Don't ask why."

"Don't ask why God didn't intervene—it's not our place to question God."


## "God in a Box"

God only needs to be approached correctly—*then* He'll do what you want. Right?

"If you pray the right way, God will hear you," people say. But is that the true character of God?

"God will *have* to make good on His word. Pray this verse over your terminally ill husband and God will *have* to heal him."

God *is* as good as His word, that's true. He *is* faithful to perform His word—*His word*, not ours. Twisting Scripture makes it our word, not His.

We are tempted to believe that if we say all the right words and if we can manage to do all the right things, God is obligated to bend His will to ours. It's as simple as this; if I impress Him, He will accommodate me. Such a subtle lie has worked itself even into the Christian message.


## God's Plan Is Not Necessarily Our Plan

God's will is more than just finding a way through the maze of decisions and options we face throughout life. It is more than just finding out how He views certain issues and voting with Him on those issues. God's will is the destiny He has prescribed for each one of our lives. It is the purpose He has tucked within the spirits of His children. It is the sense of fulfillment we experience when we are moving in unity with Him as we labor to build His kingdom within the hearts of people. It is knowing His heart toward the hurting, His plan for drawing people to himself, and His mind about how we are to run our churches, our lives, and how we treat the members of our families.

It can be astonishing to realize that *God's will is often more a lifestyle than a road map.*

Consider these points from Colossians 1:9–12.

"For this reason, since the day we heard about you, we have not stopped praying for you and asking God to fill you with the knowledge of His will through all spiritual wisdom and understanding. And we pray this in order that you may live a life worthy of the Lord and may please Him in every way: bearing fruit in every good work, growing in the knowledge of God, being strengthened with all power according to His glorious might so that you may have great endurance and patience, and joyfully giving thanks to the Father, who has qualified you to share in the inheritance of the saints in the kingdom of light."

1. *God's will includes the desire to come to a full understanding of His purpose.* He wants you to know what He's about. He wants to show you what He's doing in and through you and why. He wants a relationship with you.

2. *God's will is not just about doing, but being—living in the place of His will.* Ephesians 2:6–7 says: "And God raised us up with Christ and seated us with Him in the heavenly realms in Christ Jesus, in order that in the coming ages He might show the incomparable riches of His grace, expressed in His kindness to us in Christ Jesus." God's will is as much positional as it is practical. Living *in* Him, positionally must even come before living *for* Him.

We have found His will when we find our life in Him.

3. *Recognizing the power of His will.* We think of God's power mainly as dynamic and explosive. But His power is also contained in the sweet quietness of experiencing His grace. His will is to understand the power of His resurrection life, coursing through your veins, giving you life and strength. The power of His will is seen in a tiny bud giving promise early in the spring of full ripened fruit coming in the fall. The power of His will is demonstrated as much in patience as it is in spiritual warfare—maybe more.

We can be filled with the knowledge of His will in all spiritual wisdom and understanding—not just the *what*, but the *why*! Why is this such an abstract concept to so many? Perhaps it's the fleshly, *can-do* spirit that makes us so ready to believe God's will is something you *do*. We don't understand the concept of *being* first, then doing. Perhaps it's because so many of us have only found our being in what we do, not what or who we are.

Maybe it's difficult to grasp the *being* concept of God's will because it requires relationship. A relationship that involves time and personal investment. It necessitates intimacy and honesty. And, what a shame it's so misunderstood. Because it's so simple, really. God's will happens within the context of a relationship with Him. It's not something you do for God, it's something you do *in* Him, and He accomplishes within you.

One day I (Neva) was speaking to a group of ladies at a retreat especially designed for the overweight. These discouraged and defeated women needed desperately to know they were okay with God, even if they were less (or more) than what society calls acceptable.

"How much does God want me to weigh?" one of them tearfully asked. "I want to please Him so much. What is His will for my ideal weight?"

"Can you imagine yourself sitting at the feet of the Lord, much like Mary when He visited her home?" I asked her.

"Oh yes," she responded. "It is my favorite mental picture of being in relationship and prayer with Jesus."

"If you were to close your eyes, then, you would be able to see the setting?"

"Of course," she said.

"Is it your house?"

"Yes, it's my living room. In front of the big window. I like to think of Christ sitting in the big chair there, and me sitting on the floor in front of Him. In fact, I often have my daily devotional time there. It makes it seem so much more personal."

"Then, close your eyes and picture this for me. Now tell me, sitting right there in front of the Lord, how much do you weigh?"

"I can't tell," she said.

"Oh?"

"No, I can see me, but I seem to have no size."

"Do you know where you're sitting?"

"Sure. At His feet."

"So you know—" before I could finish she interrupted me.

"His will for me is not a size, it's a place!" Her eyes brimmed with tears. "You know one of the reasons I like to sit there with Him every day is because as long as I'm there, and in His presence, my weight is not the issue, my heart is."

Is that how we have been taught to look for God's will?

Probably not. We look for God's will by looking for actions, not understanding that answers come *within* God's will. We ask for specific direction, thinking God's will is in specifics. Yet, God's will within our hearts and directing our lives daily by the principles of His word provide many of the specifics we pray for so diligently.

We try to "prove" God's will, or press for it to be revealed by trying out solutions to our problems. In other words, we attempt to find a solution or gain a level of security on our own terms, often getting ahead of God. We complain, "Then just show me what to do!" What God may really want is to make us into what He wants us to be, so that what we do comes *naturally* out of our character—a character changed by His working in our lives, and by His Word as it enables us to move and think and decide according to His life as it works within us.

Don't you agree that it would be most exciting and peaceful to live knowing God's will is working within you? Can you imagine such a life?

The need to make a decision approaches. A direction has to be chosen. God's will is being worked within, and the decision is made with ease. Success in Christ is sure. How can that be?

First, living within God's will, and God's will being worked within helps you to remember that choice is a God-given responsibility. We have security by staying close to the Lord, remaining confident even in His occasional silence. He is still working. We find the comfort of letting God work through the details rather than feeling we have to manipulate the situation to assure it comes out the way we want it to. How freeing it would be to concentrate on staying within God's boundaries, focusing on being safely within God's parameters for blessing and protection, according to the instructions in His Word. Aware of the problems, surely, but concentrating on His principles instead. Peacefully accepting God's terms, letting Him open and close doors to make things happen according to His will and purpose. Living out His will, living in His will, seeking His favor and face, and experiencing His grace. Empowered to live His will—simply, naturally.

Does this sound too good to be true? It can happen. I (Zane) have seen it for myself in the lives of two men I greatly admire and respect—John Michael Talbot, and pastor-missionary Leroy Cloud.

John Michael Talbot lives a simple life, free of encumbrances. He makes sure his life is uncluttered and unfettered in order to be readily available and portable. John has chosen to plant no roots in this life, making him always available to kingdom affairs and business. Totally tuned to the Lord's will within him, he remains ready to go or ready to stay—ready in an instant, should God need Him in another place.

Pastor Cloud isn't as portable, but he is just a pliable to the Lord's will working within him. As a young pastor under his leadership, I often heard him expound on the importance of living daily Romans 12:1–2, which says:

"Therefore, I urge you, brothers, in view of God's mercy, to offer your bodies as living sacrifices, holy and pleasing to God—this is your spiritual act of worship. Do not conform any longer to the pattern of this world, but be transformed by the renewing of your mind. Then you will be able to test and approve what God's will is—His good, pleasing and perfect will."

Pastor Cloud emphasized continually the importance of being a world-free, non-conformist. Not in a rebellious or reckless sense, but in freedom from pressure of popular opinion. He has modeled for me what it is like to live a life of spiritual worship. He has let me have access to his transformed, renewed mind and see for myself a man who truly flows within the will of God because the will of God flows within him. It is no strain for Pastor Cloud to make a decision, to face a crossroads or to be presented with an unusual choice. With grace and ease he flows within God's will and brings God's will to the circumstance rather than looking for God's will in the circumstance. "If you wait until the decision has to be made before you know God's will," his life says, "you have waited too long to know God's will." In other words, it's not God's will in the situation—it's God's will *in me*!

It's no wonder people seek out a counselor at a crossroads moment and ask questions like: Which way do I turn? Where do I go from here? How could this have happened to me? Why me? What should I do now? And, How can I find the mind of the Lord on this? Those who have never gotten in touch with knowing God's will as it is being worked out within them react to circumstances rather than respond.

Those who respond to God's will on a daily basis respond to His will when crossroads choices have to be made. With plenty of time spent in God's presence, responders have had lots of preparation for life's surprises and unexpected circumstances. Why? Because rather than internalize or simply live with a reflex motion when problems arise, or externalize and react in panic or complaint, responders *eternalize* their experiences.

To *eternalize* is not to be mistaken for *spiritualizing*—that is, tossing around Christian phrases and verbiage to explain everything that comes down the pike. To *eternalize* is to have the ability not only to look at but *through* the event toward the spiritual crossroads it presents.

For instance, when a responder is faced with a crossroads experience like a job change, he knows that more is at stake than just a job. He knows he also stands at another crossroads, possibly more important than the job. Trust and faith are tested. Will he rely on God, or take things into his own hands? Will he take the time to consider his options, or go with the first good-sounding prospect that comes along. Will he *rest* once he has made his decision, before he announces it to the family or his boss? In other words, a responder lets the sun come up a time or two, even after he makes his decision—but before he takes any action.

A responder verbalizes his requests, but also listens for answers when he prays about his crossroads events. He refuses to give up hope, no matter how bleak the outlook, because what's at the real crossroads is not the outlook, but his eternal outcome—how he will let the circumstance deepen his trust and intimacy with God.

A responder knows his crossroads event presents him with another crossroads. Will he praise God through this situation? Will he continue to sing and make melody in his heart in spite of how dark the day? Will he keep on serving, tending to the needs of others, even when his own needs are so apparent? Will he retreat on the defensive, or will he continue to attack enemy lines as part of the offensive team? Will he wait? Will he actively, purposely determine to stay out of the way and let God work, not procrastinating or hoping it will go away or solve itself?

A responder knows to keep pressing for answers. He knows to knock and keep on knocking, to keep on seeking and to keep on looking. Not to pressure God, but to keep himself constantly alert, to be aware when the answer comes.

A responder knows there is more at stake than an answer to his problem. His trust is being tested, his faith being exercised, and his hope constantly being challenged. His situation may be financial or physical or directional, but his crossroads is relational. Basing his trust not on the changing circumstance, but on God who never changes!

And a responder perseveres. Keeps on trusting, keeps on waiting, keeps on believing no matter what. Furthermore, a responder doesn't keep to himself. A responder seeks out the counsel of other responders—not to lean, but to learn.

A person responding to God's will being worked within him begins to speak the language of a responder. "God's got an answer," he says. He even prays in this new language saying, "Lord, what do you want to teach me through this?"

"This will pass," the responder encourages friends and family. "Let's keep our eyes on the Lord. This is not the end of hope, we still have a future beyond this situation. Someday we'll all be in heaven discussing what we learned through this. Besides, we've got some good friends who know how to pray, let's ask them what they think." Always optimistic, responders know the whole world doesn't revolve around the problem they are dealing with at the moment. While they wait for the Lord's will to be revealed within them, they look for where they can be of most use. Yes, responders find ways to serve while they wait. "In the meantime," they say, "while we wait we can . . ." They face difficulty with courage, knowing tough doesn't necessarily mean impossible. They know it may be hard—"But soon," they say, "we'll see what God is doing."

Successful crossroads navigators are God's-will people. They know deep within their hearts that God is up to something.

That's all there is to it.

# 18

# Do You Hear What I Hear?

---

### Purpose #2

**Determine to become a "listener," not just a "hearer," settling once and for all the fact that God's Word becomes real to us only when we do it.**

---

The young mother placed her hand firmly on the shoulder of her first-grader. "Didn't you hear me? I said, go get your sister." Can't we all remember parents who said, "Are you listening?"

Funny thing, the parent who asks such a question is not really referring to the ability to hear audible sound. The parent who asks, "Didn't you hear me?" is addressing behavior. The implication is, "If you hear me, you will do what I ask."

In the Old Testament, we find these words:

"Does the LORD delight in burnt offerings and sacrifices as

much as in obeying the voice of the LORD? To obey is better than sacrifice, and to heed is better than the fat of rams."[1]

In this use of the word "obey," the meaning is "to hear, to act upon." In this sense, "obeying" and "hearing" are expressed by exactly the same word. When God says to us, "hear me," He is also saying, "obey me in what you hear." So then, we can accurately say that, in the biblical sense of the word, "to obey means to hear and respond in a conforming action"— involving both hearing and doing.

All throughout the Bible, there are verses that say much the same thing: "Obey the voice of the Lord." The implication is clear, the voice of the Lord can be clearly heard and, furthermore, it can be understood and it is to be complied with.

Can you hear the Lord's voice? Do you do what you know He is speaking to you? How does God confirm His Word to you?

When you and I face crossroads experiences, it is important that we have already developed a responsive ear—an ear tuned to the voice of the Lord.

## Does God "Speak" Today?

There is a question in the minds of some today about whether or not God really speaks to us individually. If so, how does He speak? And how can we hear Him?

In an earlier chapter we talked about "power voices" that clamor for attention within all of us. We encouraged you to get familiar with them and be able to tell them from the one true voice of power—God's voice. This chapter takes that thought one step further, going beyond just being able to distinguish God's voice from all the other voices or influences in your life, and finding the strength to obey what He says.

The Scriptures are very clear that God does indeed speak to us, that He has always spoken to us.

In Genesis 1, it is recorded *eleven* times that God spoke the very world and all that we see and enjoy into existence. Throughout the Old Testament, it is repeatedly recorded— God spoke to His people.

He spoke to them through prophets and through priests. He spoke to them through angels, dreams, and visions. But the

---

[1] 1 Samuel 15:22

point is: God is a speaking God—and we can hear Him.

Many people are very confused as to *how* God speaks. Some expect the voice of God to boom out of heaven and tell them detail by detail how to live their lives. Not that God couldn't do that should He choose, but for the most part God has chosen to speak to His people gently and in very ordinary ways.

Sometimes He speaks to us through plain old-fashioned *common sense.*

Sometimes we come to the knowledge that particular habits or lifestyle practices are unhealthy. Some practices and habits cause sickness, disease, and death. Then we read words like:

"This day I call heaven and earth as witnesses against you that I have set before you life and death, blessings and curses. Now choose life, so that you and your children may live and that you may love the LORD your God, listen to His voice, and hold fast to Him. For the LORD is your life, and He will give you many years in the land He swore to give to your fathers, Abraham, Isaac, and Jacob."[2]

It becomes perfectly clear what the Lord is saying. Don't do the things you *know* lead to death. Choose life. Do our lifestyle choices demonstrate that we have heard God speak in this way?

Other times, God speaks to us confirming what we sense in our heart through a passage of scripture. For example, if you have been facing a decision, and all you have to go on is that inner compass drawing you toward a particular direction, you make your decision prayerfully and openly before God. Of course, you realize that you won't stumble across a verse that says, "Yes, my child, that Chevy is the right choice." It is not unusual, following a decision, to have a verse from the Bible leap out during devotions or a sermon. It seems to say, "My child, you have chosen the right way," or "Yes, this is for you," or "No, not now."

Psalm 138:8 has been a verse that my life (Neva) has actually hinged upon for almost twenty years:

"The LORD will fulfill His purpose for me; your love, O LORD, endures forever—do not abandon the works of your hands."

---

[2]Deuteronomy 30:19–20

No matter what has come and gone, struggles or pressures, pain or disappointment, I have known that above it all, God has a purpose bigger and stronger even than my pain or failure—a purpose that cannot be quenched by temporary circumstance. A friend gave me this verse one time when I was confused and seeking direction. It gave me the courage to wait, to let Him work, and the hope that no matter what, God had chosen to be involved in my life and would continue to do so.

This verse came at a time when I was following what I believed to be very strict obedience in even the smallest details of my life and daily habits. And it stayed with me during days when I wanted nothing to do with being disciplined and obedient. It continued to provide promise, even when I failed God and myself. It remained burned into my heart whenever I wanted to give up hope. God had spoken, and He wasn't taking it back.

God may speak to you through a friend or your spouse. He might use your doctor, your pastor, or even your children to get His message across. And He will always confirm—that is, He will *underline* that what you have heard is or isn't from Him—from His Word.

God also speaks to us through experience. Lessons learned in the furnace are seldom forgotten. Did Daniel ever forget that God could close the mouths of hungry lions or question whether or not God could protect him? Did God have to gather dark clouds in the sky in order to get Noah's attention after the flood? Firsthand experience with God's power leaves us with the distinct memory that He has spoken.

Though God may sometimes appear to be silent, He is still a speaking God! He not only hears, but answers! We long to hear Him speak, but are we willing to listen to what He says? Are we willing to "heed" the voice of the Lord?

In addition to a responsive ear, listening to God's voice means we develop a listening heart.

This journey we call life is taken under the leadership of our Lord, Jesus Christ. Once we accept Him as Savior, He steps into the position of guide, protector, corrector, and forgiver. He shows us His ways, instills within us the principles of His Word and changes us from the inside out. A lifestyle of obedience is how we express a responsive ear and a listening heart. The psalmist knew such a life when he penned:

"I have set the LORD always before me. Because He is at my

right hand, I will not be shaken. Therefore my heart is glad and my tongue rejoices; my body also will rest secure, because you will not abandon me to the grave, nor will you let your Holy One see decay. You have made known to me the path of life; you will fill me with joy in your presence, with eternal pleasures at your right hand."[3]

A lifestyle of listening is not the same as a life riddled with rules, but rather a life lived in relationship with the Ruler. It is not lived meticulously according to the law, but in loving relationship with the Lawgiver. In the same way, it is not a life dependent on the gifts of the Holy Spirit, but on the Holy Spirit himself.

Lest we give you the impression that hearing from God is simple and comes easy, let us assure you, it isn't always so. It can be very perilous to simply assume because someone says, "God said . . ." that He really "said . . ." We need checkpoints to confirm or verify that, indeed, He has spoken:

1. Always be alert for confirmation through a second person. God has always worked through the entire body of Christ—not just a few. In fact, it was only when His people were in full-blown rebellion that He used individual prophets. Look at the many authors used to write the Bible as a living illustration of how God uses many to speak His Word. Listen to those whom God has placed over you in places of spiritual authority as a place for a word to be confirmed. Listen to those with whom you live in close community—who know you better than anyone else—as a valid resource for confirmation. Simply remember this, if God said it once, He can say it again.[4]

2. Confirmation also comes within the heart. When God speaks, especially concerning major decisions or directions, He places it in the heart, not just the head. For those who are married, it is best to delay moving on a "word from God" requiring a decision until it is confirmed in both hearts.

3. Wait for the fulfillment of the word of the Lord before you act on it. In more earthly terms, don't spend the *Reader's Digest* Sweepstakes jackpot *before* the check is safely deposited in your account. If God says He is going to bless and prosper you, let Him do it before you run the charge cards to their

---

[3]Psalm 16:8–11

[4]This and subsequent points are based in part on an excellent article, "When They Say, 'God Told Me,' " by Ross Lakes, *Leadership* Magazine, Winter Quarter, 1985.

limits or drive the luxury car off the showroom floor.

4. Don't assume that because you have heard the Lord speak, He wants it announced immediately. Let the word of the Lord season within your spirit. Keep it bathed in prayer and cultivated in obedience. Live in what you already know to obey in and let Him expand His word within the context of your present walk. While a word from the Lord may require that you abandon a dream or a plan, it never requires that you abandon responsibility or reason.

5. Whenever God calls, He enables. Whatever He says is possible to obey.

"Now what I am commanding you today is not too difficult for you or beyond your reach. It is not up in heaven, so that you have to ask, 'Who will ascend into heaven to get it and proclaim it to us so we may obey it?' Nor is it beyond the sea, so that you have to ask, 'Who will cross the sea to get it and proclaim it to us so we may obey it?' No, the word is very near you; it is in your mouth and in your heart so you may obey it."[5]

But, you may be saying, if God is speaking, why can't we simply throw caution to the winds and with abandon obey His voice? You can, once you are sure it *is* His voice. To do anything less would be at the least foolish and at the most disobedience. Obey only when you are *biblically* sure it is His voice. You see, as Ross Lakes put it, "It's because of the pipeline through which they come" that we need to be so careful of "words from the Lord."

God's communication skills are perfect. Our listening skills—to put it mildly—need some improvement.

And besides, should we really expect God to say anything else to us if we're not obeying Him in what we've already heard quite clearly?

Successful crossroads navigators have learned far in advance of crossroads experiences that essential listening skills need to be honed and perfected. How do they do that? Watch some you know. Observe their lives. You will see lives that are marked by a response to God's will within, and an obedience to that will. Successful crossroads navigators have this wonderful determination about them! They are determined not only to hear God's voice, but to heed what they hear.

---

[5]Deuteronomy 30:11–14

They *do* what they hear God speak much more than they *repeat* what God has said to them. Having settled it once and for all, successful crossroads navigators demonstrate the truth that God's Word is more than heard—it's done.

And when crossroads experiences come, as they do to all of us, the successful crossroads navigator doesn't plow his way through. Nor does he muddle around in confusion and fear. He *listens* his way through—in a quietly doing, obedient way.

# 19

# Spiritual Health Care Reform

---

## Purpose #3
### Maintain spiritual health.

---

Most everyone is familiar with the health care programs called HMO's. They are the Health Maintenance Organizations that have been competing with the more traditional medical insurance plans for the last several years. It was the HMO who first began the emphasis on wellness being as important to preventing illness as medical care is to curing it. Whether or not you agree with the way HMO's work, or manage their patients, their stated philosophies serve as worthy models for understanding the importance of personal responsibility as it relates to individual health.

These same philosophies would be nothing less than revolutionary if we applied them spiritually.

For example, what if the church served as your Spiritual Health Maintenance Organization, Jesus Christ as your Primary Care Physician and your pastor as the Physician's Assistant? With such qualified caregivers would you worry or concern yourself with maintaining your own spiritual health? You should, for many reasons.

You see, there is more to providing good spiritual health care than just being there when you have a need or a crisis. Weddings and funerals, baby dedications and baptisms are only part of the Christian's life. Most of us face life in the middle lane, if not in the fast lane. We go to work every day, pay bills every month, and mow our lawns each Saturday. As strange as it seems, it is in the everyday routine that our faith is tested and stretched far more than in our "religious" activities or even the crisis experiences. Crossroads come to us in the day to day, they are the rule, not the exception. And we must be ready.

If we have a spiritual health problem, it may *surface* at church, but it rarely *starts* there. It is the same with spiritual wellness. It may be encouraged at church, even taught there in classes and Bible studies. But wellness only happens when certain spiritually healthy practices are carried out at home, at work, and in our community involvement.

Living a healthy life means different things to different people. Yet, we can see a common thread running through those whose lives are healthy and who manage to stay healthy. That thread is balance. Successful crossroads navigators demonstrate balance in their daily spiritual health habits.

Finding the right balance in all the different dimensions of life—physically, emotionally, and spiritually—is called "wellness." And wellness is something we can all achieve.

Though the church may offer a number of "wellness" programs and classes, good spiritual health really begins at home. Just as you would visit your local medical clinic for vision and hearing exams, you come for vision and hearing screening at church or through reading Christian materials and books. You might take a class series on Christian marriage and relationships, but unless you practice the wealth of healthy information you receive at home, you will soon find your marriage or relationships suffering.

If you are to have a head start on being spiritually healthy, you will need to know what's healthy and what's not. But more than that, you will need to know how to maintain your spiritual health regardless of what's happening at work, at church, or even in your home life. This enables you to manage balance toward a healthy spiritual lifestyle, whether you are facing a crossroads, navigating a crossroads, or recovering from a crossroads experience.

While those in leadership of your Spiritual Health Maintenance Organization—your church—have pooled their resources and talents together to provide the members with the best in spiritual health care services, you will get the biggest benefit from belonging *if* your personal emphasis is on prevention, not just the cure of spiritual illness. If spiritual wellness becomes your priority, belonging to a church means you will become a contributor, a giver, not just an attender and a receiver. You become a part of a spiritual health care team— not just attend church week to week, much like a chronically ill patient who regularly needs to see his doctor.

Your spiritual health is up to you. And it can be managed starting in your own home. It's up to you.

## Maintaining a Spiritually Healthy Perspective

You've probably heard that stress is bad for you. But stress can be good for you. Too much is distressing, a little is a blessing. What does it all mean? Stress is life, life is stress.

It's strange, but stress can be one person's spiritual downfall, and another's spiritual motivation. Even Christians sometimes experience stress-related physical symptoms. Insomnia, depression, headaches, or stomach upsets are often connected to stress and indicate a need to manage stress more effectively.

Spiritually, the symptoms of stress often differ from person to person. Criticism, complaining, back-biting and lack of interest in spiritual things can be symptoms of stressed-out Christians. Indifference, passivity, and neglect of God's Word often are due to the lack of balanced spiritually healthy practices, and promote even more spiritual stress, leading to a maddening and discouraging cycle of spiritual health decline.

Just as in the physical realm, we can learn to manage spiritual stress. The key to bringing the stress in your life to a manageable level is balance—so too, spiritually. To use the key, we must strategize. Following are several practical Spiritual Health Management (SHM) strategies you could use.

## SHM Strategy Number One: Avoid, eliminate, or substitute for stressful situations

If fighting crowds at the mall drives you crazy, consider avoiding the stress by shopping from catalogs, over the phone, or during off-peak hours. Spiritually, if serving on committees, heading departments, or teaching two-year-olds is too much for you, look for other more suitable areas of service. Do your church flower beds need weeding? Is there room for another voice in the choir? Could your pastor or one of the Sunday school teachers use a research assistant? Could the nursery use new curtains or crib sheets? Are there jobs for volunteers in the church office? Do the windowsills need repainting? Is there a shut-in or new mother who would benefit from a home-cooked and personally delivered hot meal? Out-front leadership isn't the only place for effective service.

## SHM Strategy Number Two: Learn to cope with and manage stressful situations

Some things can't or shouldn't be avoided. Maybe you have made a commitment to teach the two-year-olds for the entire term. It's only February, and your term isn't up until the second week in June, but your class has grown from a delightful three to an unmanageable fifteen. You know you are responsible to complete what you have begun, so it's important then to *manage* the situation and cope with the stress. Decide if there is anything you can change about the situation to make it more manageable.

I (Neva) am responsible for the decorations and visual seasonal changes at my church. During the times when I am pressured with writing deadlines, overwhelmed by family responsibilities, and challenged with the needs of the other areas of ministry, I have to find ways to manage the stress. Otherwise I am taxed beyond my physical and spiritual limits. So, I find helpers. It's as simple as that. I have sought out the artistic people of our congregation—the seamstresses, those with an eye for display, and people who aren't afraid to climb ladders—and I delegate. I find making banners on small pieces of paper and handing them to Bonnie, our banner person, is far easier than trying to do it all myself. Jody also sews banners, and Sheila loves to display them. Marilyn has a good eye for balance, and although she can't help a lot physically, she encourages and gives good, clear suggestions. (She also is wise enough to look the other way when her husband, Sid, climbs the ladder to hang the Christmas wreath higher than anyone else can.) Kathy and Del make stringing lights a party, and Candi adds a special touch of elegance to anything she touches. I manage, but not alone.

Once in a while, a situation comes up that can't be avoided or eliminated. When a substitute won't do and the situation refuses to be managed, another strategy is needed.

## SHM Strategy Number Three: Let go

Does this sound too simple? If a situation is entirely out of control, we need to learn to let go. Ask yourself, "How important will this issue or project be in five minutes, five hours, or five months?" Will it make a difference or will anyone even remember it in five years? Perspective can sometimes only be gained if we're willing to let go.

Letting go doesn't mean we quit. It may not even mean we get to take our hands off, it only means we learn to turn loose. Simply, it means we let go of our expectations. We let go of having it go entirely our own way. We let go of our perfectionistic tendencies and do the best we can, even though it may not be the best job possible. We give it all we've got, then humbly offer it to the Lord as our best offering. And when we do, we regain our balance.

## SHM Strategy Number Four: Rest

The world would say, "Cool it." Stretching, deep breathing, warm baths, getting together with friends, or digging in the garden are all effective strategies for dealing with physical and emotional stress. Spiritually we might add the occasional need to retreat. Sometimes right in the thick of it, the smartest move we can make is to take a break. Take a mini-retreat and sit in the yard, just to be quiet before God. Take a drive to a place where you can see the horizon off in the distance—walk beside the sea or the river—climb a tree if necessary, but find a place where you can rest for a moment.

Even more important, *cast all the care of your stressful situation on Christ.* The Bible says you can cast your care on Him for He cares for you.[1] How simple this concept becomes when we read the verse with one simple accentuated adjustment: "Cast all your cares and anxieties on Him, for He cares *for* you." Let Him carry the care *for* you. You'll be surprised how quickly the pattern of spiritual fatigue and tension can be broken when we let Him do the care carrying.

## SHM Strategy Number Five: Bring spiritual balance by making time for the three R's:

*Recover.* After any major change in your life, you need time to recover. It is the same spiritually. When there has been a death, birth, divorce, or personal crisis, we need to recover. Too many people try to pick up immediately and try to go on without missing a step when some of the severest of life's challenges hit. It's as if they alone have to prove that God's grace is sufficient without spending time processing healthy grief or making a full recovery. A weekend getaway, a quiet personal retreat, or just a leave of absence from certain responsibilities can be a healthy way to plan for recovery. It's okay to admit you need distance to regain perspective and to consider options. Stepping back to look at the big picture, you'll be able to have greater peace about the change or decision you need to make.

*Refocus.* Don't run away, but from a little distance, think about the changes occurring in your life. Consider how it may affect the rest of your life. Talk to friends, family, or a counselor. Recognize and realize that during stressful times feelings are often mixed, even for consistent, solid people. Feelings are feelings. They are genuine emotions. Even if they are rather poor navigational instruments, they can be excellent inner warning devices. Spending time in God's Word, studying the lives of people who have also been thrown into change and forced to make adjustments is a wonderful resource for man-

---

[1] 1 Peter 5:7. "Cast all your anxiety on Him because He cares for you."

aging spiritual health and making biblical choices and decisions.

*Regenerate.* Spiritual regeneration began when we accepted Christ as personal Savior. It continues as we turn to Him as our Shepherd and Lord. Nothing recharges spiritual batteries faster than a season waiting at His feet. Prayer doesn't always have to be spent in words and warfare, it can be spent quietly soaking in His presence. Submit yourself *for* prayer as well as spend time *in* prayer. I (Zane) meet with the elders of my congregation on a regular basis. I don't take the complete responsibility for the spiritual direction and ministry solely upon my own shoulders. I submit myself for prayer regularly with these godly men.

I (Neva) submit myself for prayer often on Sunday morning before the regular worship service. In our church, we have a prayer room staffed with trained people who care and understand those of us who come for prayer each week. I find such prayer ministry sustaining when I'm working on a book project, considering a change in direction, or before I begin a new responsibility or face a personal challenge. It's not that I don't regularly pray for myself, but there is a regenerating effect upon my life and work when I regularly submit for the prayer ministry of other believers.

Regeneration also happens when we increase our circle of support. Connecting with new people, reinforcing old friendships, brings refreshing balance to our lives. Finding balance is a day to day responsibility. Getting sufficient rest, avoiding destructive habits such as cigarettes and alcohol and poor eating choices, help us manage our spiritual as much as our physical health.

## It's Up to You

Recovery, refocus, and regeneration help us to change as our circumstances change.

Look at those who you consider successful crossroads navigators. Do you see some of the Spiritual Health Management strategies at work in their lives? Probably so. Strategies you can incorporate as well.

Your physical health maintenance doesn't depend as much on your doctor as it does on you. He can diagnose your illness and sometimes give you pills that will help, but you have to be faithful to take them. He can give you advice, but you have to follow it. You can make decisions that enhance your physical well-being, or choose habits and practices that destroy it. It's up to you.

In the same way, your spiritual health is also your responsibility. You can't depend totally on your pastor or the spiritual leadership of your church or Bible study for every morsel of "spiritual food" you ingest. He isn't there every day to see to it that you have your daily quiet time. He can't make sure you spend time in prayer and quietness before the Lord. He can't choose your TV programming, your reading material, or the music you listen to. That's your job. You are the one who makes the decisions that enhance or negatively affect your life spiritually.

*It's up to you.*

If you have chosen to make some positive changes toward being more spiritually responsible, here are some tips that may help.

*1. Prepare for the morning the night before.* If you want to begin to have a morning devotional time, select your material ahead of time and have it ready, on the table (with your glasses if necessary), the night before.

Make other preparations as well. Lay out your clothes, make lunches, gather the children's schoolwork, and set the table for breakfast the night before. Eliminate as much stressful rush from the morning as possible. Then, set the alarm half an hour earlier and go to bed earlier as well.

*2. Keep notes.* It's a waste of time and energy to try to keep things in your head. Keep a simple notebook or journal of the scriptures you read. In your journal write out simple prayers of insights gained during your quiet time. Note a characteristic you want to see developed or changed. Record prayers answered. Make other lists as needs that come to your attention. Groceries that need to be picked up after work. Calls that need to be made. Errands you need to run.

If you're not used to keeping notes on a daily basis, remember, it is balance we're after. A purse or pocket calendar with a day or week at a glance might be all you need to begin with. Don't make it so hard you can't keep it up. After all, going overboard doesn't make up for years of neglect, nor does it bring balance when it is too hard to continue.

*3. Organize.* Your day, your energy, your goals will all benefit from a touch of organization. Write down ten things you want to see changed or accomplished in your home, church, or workplace. Cross off five of those you cannot do anything about. Of the remaining five ask yourself even if it is possible, are you the one that *should* bring about the needed or desired change. Cross off any that aren't appropriate for you. If they are all crossed off, make another list and begin again, until you have about three to five things that you could, even should, be involved with. Be happy if you can manage two or three.

*4. Plan ahead.* Untended details often bog us down when we need to be free to respond immediately to a need or request. Gas in the tank, food in the fridge, and a supply of stamps on hand don't seem to be very spiritual. But think of being called in the night to attend a sick friend or help in a crisis—you don't want to have to pump gas then. Food in the fridge means you can invite that new couple over for lunch after church; stamps on hand means you can send a note of encouragement whenever the Holy Spirit nudges. A little cash in your wallet wouldn't hurt either. Small change in your pocket means you could impulsively treat a troubled teen to conversation over a coke and fries.

*5. Celebrate.* Life's little successes and joys are important enough to merit celebration. Christians have cause to celebrate. Redeemed, full of purpose and hope, we ought to be able to count our blessings readily, be thankful continually, and rejoice at the drop of a hat. Life and success, no longer depending upon our performance but on God's grace and mercy, is reason enough to rejoice—don't you agree?

*6. Laugh.* No one has more reasons to laugh than we do. From our joy-filled Christian perspective, we can learn to laugh even at those things formerly thought of as no laughing matter. For example, when you get right down to it, nothing is funnier than the accusations the devil makes. Absolutely hilarious are the doubts he throws at our faith, the lies he tells about our character, and the rumors he spreads about our church. He tries to make us believe that evil is about to take over the world even when Christ has already overcome it. He plots to convince us that Christ has forgotten us even though we know He's coming for us soon.

No one has more reason to have fun than we do. Almost any challenge has a humorous side to it. The Christian's sense of humor is sharpened as his spiritual health is maintained.

Vibrant and witty, believers get together to cheer favorite sports teams, play practical jokes on one another, and good-naturedly poke fun. Fortieth birthdays are meant for "roasting" someone we all love. And retreats and family camps are spent playing, not just praying together.

Laughing refreshes not only the physical body by exercising internal organs, relaxing facial muscles, and releasing chemical endorphins, but it refreshes the spirit as well. Joy springs forth in laughter. Hope's flame is rekindled when we have a good laugh; depression lifts. Laughter is like raising the window shade of our souls and letting pure, warm sunshine into our hearts.

Look again at the successful crossroads navigators you know. They look spiritually healthy and fit. Even if they suffer physically, they seem to be able to manage a healthy outlook and optimism. And it's all because, no matter what, they have made it their purpose to manage their own spiritual health. They have accepted the responsibility to define and realize their own spiritual growth goals. They go through a daily routine of lifting the weight of the cross, exercising their faith, maintaining a daily regimen of healthy food supplements from God's Word, and belonging to a church that sees itself as a Spiritual Health Maintenance Organization. Their Primary Care Physician is Jesus and they make routine visits—not just when they're sick or in trouble, but when they're well and everything's going fine. Prevention of spiritual health problems is their personal and primary emphasis.

This kind of spiritual health doesn't happen by accident—it's deliberate. It's done strategically, developed with purpose, for a purpose—to live successfully as a Christian. Isn't that your goal as well?

Are you interested in being spiritually healthy? Such health beckons, success is right around the corner. All it takes is a purposeful effort toward Spiritual Health Care Reform. What are you waiting for?

# 20

# Faith: Due Process of Prayer

---

### Purpose #4

### Accept the responsibility to maintain
### your faith.

---

"Can I come and see you?" I could hear the tears, even in her voice.

"What's going on?" I asked.

"I just need prayer."

"Oh." I wondered what had brought my friend to this point.

"I don't know how else to say it. I just need you to pray for me."

"I see."

"It's just that—well, I don't think I have the faith to believe God right now. I'm afraid. I can't bungle this up. This is too important. Please, will you pray for me?"

It's not an unusual request. Christians ask for prayer every day. We believe in the power of prayer and see the benefit of praying for one another. But have we carried it too far? Do we ask for prayer when we need to do the praying ourselves?

It's quite common for those in need to ask for prayer. There are genuine, appropriate times for the body of Christ to lift one of its own before the Lord in prayer—but on a regular basis, for the everyday issues?

Successful crossroads navigators seem to ask for prayer less frequently than most people. Does that mean they have lost faith? Certainly not. Does that mean they no longer believe in the power of prayer? Hardly.

Successful crossroads navigators have simply determined to be responsible to manage their own faith. By that we mean, they have made the commitment to go through the process of building and maintaining their own faith. This often means they come to church or prayer group with their prayers already prayed, assured the answers are already on the way. They may respond when the opportunity is given for ministry and encouragement, grateful to have others stand with them in faith. But they don't depend on the group for faith. How did they do it? They have made the effort, disciplined themselves, and accepted the responsibility to maintain their own faith.

They come with their future securely fastened down, their hope connected tightly to God's Word, and their lives anchored firmly on a solid foundation. And they did it through the due process of prayer. In other words, a solid faith, birthed and bathed in prayer. And their prayers show it. Listen to them pray. Their prayers are also birthed and bathed in faith.

Faith and prayer. Prayer and faith. It's difficult to draw a distinction between them. And, no wonder, for they are intertwined so tightly that without one, you no longer have the other. But since we have explored the concepts of prayer in earlier chapters, let's look at faith more closely.

## Faith Is More Than a Belief . . .

No matter who you ask, you may get a slightly different definition of faith. The dictionary simply says that faith is an unquestioning belief. That faith is anything believed. As you can see, if our faith is strictly something we believe without question, then faith can be a lie. Yes, it's true.

There are many right around us who believe they are worthless. They believe it even though they have received Jesus Christ as their Savior. Without question, they doubt God's judgment in sending His Son to die for someone as worthless and hopeless and unlovable as they are. Their faith, then, is actually riddled with doubt. There are others who believe, without question, that God would answer the prayers of others before He would even hear theirs. Maybe you've felt like that. *If I can just get the pastor to pray for me. If I can just get the healing evangelist to pray. If I can get my mother-in-law to pray. I know, I'll call the prayer line, then God will have to answer my prayer and meet my need.*

The point is, the dictionary definition of faith isn't enough. It isn't based on anything other than a belief. But biblical faith, active and alive faith, is based on much more.

## Faith Is More Than a Word

There are those who believe that an active and energized faith is based on the Bible. And so it is . . . sort of. They hold that you only have to find a verse that "witnesses" to your spirit—a passage that somehow connects to your need—and then the spark of hope ignited by God's Word is faith.

But living faith is so much more than searching Scripture to find a verse you can turn in to God like a coupon He's obligated to honor. Living, breathing faith is born out of relationship with Him. Living *in* Him. Hoping in Him.

## Faith Is More Than Prayer

If you would, imagine for a moment a diver walking toward a fifty-foot tower. He pauses at the bottom of the ladder and looks toward the top. Then, he begins his long climb toward the platform from which he will make his dramatic dive. Reaching the top, the diver pauses to catch his breath. The tower has a microphone and a speaker for a sports journalist to interview him as he prepares for his dive.

"How do you feel right now?" the standard reporter-type question comes across the speaker.

"A little nervous."

"How's that?"

"Well, I've never dived from this height before. My highest dive was twelve feet."

"Twelve feet? Are you sure you ought to do this?" the reporter asks.

"I'm not really sure," the diver admits.

"Then why are you?"

"Others do it all the time," the diver says. "If they can, I guess I can too."

"Tell me, how did you prepare yourself for this daring feat?"

"Well, I prayed. I really did. From the time I first put my foot on that bottom rung of the ladder all the way up to here, I prayed. I certainly did."

"And what did you pray for?"

"I prayed for the strength and courage to make this dive. And I prayed I'd live through it."

"Yeah, but this kind of high diving takes skill and technique. What makes you think you can manage this?"

"I have faith," the diver boasts. "This dive is a leap of faith." An unquestioning belief that when he leaves that platform, he can dive into the water—but he's scared to death. You and I both know, however, that his success isn't making it into the pool, but whether or not he will get out of the pool alive.

Foolish? Of course. But it happens in the lives of Christians every day. Faith-leaping from towers beyond their preparation. Then, if they survive, battered and bruised they write off faith as a hoax and prayer as a waste of time.

But faith is not a leap, it's a growing process.

## The Faith Process

Take another diver. After years of coaching and practice he has inched himself higher and higher up the side of the tower. He has studied the exact movement of the tower as it responds to his climb. He has fine tuned his senses to the breeze and how it will affect not only the tower but his body as it plummets through the air toward the water. For as many hours as he has studied diving, he has also studied the water. He knows the precise depth and every inch of the bottom of the pool. He also knows exactly how to hold his body and how he must instantly respond to the impact when he hits the water.

Even more importantly he has the best and most experienced coach in the sport and has spent countless hours alongside him watching him coach others as well. In fact, the diver has spent so much time with the coach he can sense his tension, knows when his coach is relaxed. He can tell when the coach is pleased with the tower, the platform, the weather, and the pool. Knowing his coach so well, he knows if his dive is called off it will wait for another day.

What is the difference between these two illustrations? When the first diver made his faith confession, we could see him as foolish—even suicidal. And the second? We know his faith is based on confidence and preparation built through the training of an expert coach.

## Faith Preparation

Ralph Nevis, a strong, solidly built Portuguese fellow, approached me (Zane) one day. "I hear you could use a new kitchen floor."

"Boy, could I ever!" I responded. As a young associate pastor I had been given living quarters in an old house on the edge of the church property. It was in desperate need of repair and part of my job was to repair and fix it up. Ralph was a floor covering professional. He did linoleum like an artist. I, on the other hand, was full of energy but inexperienced and green. Lacking experience, I excitedly looked forward to laying the new floor. Jan and I spent hours painting and remodeling the old house, anxious for the day to finally come when Ralph would be there to help me put in the new floor.

"Now let's get one thing straight, Anderson. I'm going to help you put in the floor, but I'm not going to do it for you."

"Good, man. Let's get started." I could barely contain my enthusiasm.

"This is going to take a couple of weeks," Ralph said.

"Two weeks? No way. I'm ready to go to it. I bet we can do this in no time at all!"

"Two weeks," he said firmly. "First thing you're going to do is rip up the old linoleum."

"Let's just lay the new stuff over the top."

"That's the problem with you young guys," he said, "you're always trying to cover the old stuff. You just want to cover it over—but I want it ripped up."

I didn't like what I was hearing at all. What Ralph was telling me was that it was going to take time and hard work.

"I want it ripped up so that in fifty years there'll still be a beautiful floor here." He looked me straight in the eye. "I don't do quick work—I do good work. Good work takes preparation."

For hours and hours, I worked ripping up the old linoleum. Then I started on the rotted subflooring. Finally under Ralph's watchful eye I began laying a new subfloor. "Can't we just get to the linoleum?"

"That's a fifteen-minute job, Zane. If you want it to last, to be beautiful for years to come, preparation is the key. Remember I don't do—"

"Yeah, I know. You don't do *quick* work. You do *good* work."

"That's right. And when you work with me—so do you."

Joints in the subfloor had to be filled, sanded, filled and sanded again. The subfloor had to be perfect and flawless. Finally, when the subfloor met with Ralph's approval we began to measure and install the new flooring. And, when it was finished, it was perfect. And Ralph was right, it wasn't quick, but it was good—really good.

It's the same with preparing our life with faith. We look for the quick fixes and easy routes. We want to lay the new strength of our belief in Christ over the old rotted flooring of our lives. But God doesn't do quick work—He does good work.

His desire is that our lives be prepared in such a way the work stays beautiful and lasts even beyond our lifetime. Strength and depth of character aren't developed without a solid subfloor perfectly prepared in faith.

## *Faith Grows in the Nitty-Gritty, Not in the Neat and Nifty.*

Day in and day out we have opportunities to prepare our lives in faith. It comes through reading the Word of God diligently[1] and praying consistently.[2] It is built when we trust God in the day to day, the ordinary and the routine issues of life.[3] Learning from Him, receiving from Him, and watching Him move not only in our own lives but also in the lives of others.

---

[1]Romans 10:17: "Consequently, faith comes from hearing the message, and the message is heard through the word of Christ."

[2]Ephesians 6:18: "And pray in the Spirit on all occasions with all kinds of prayers and requests. With this in mind, be alert and always keep on praying for all the saints."

[3]Matthew 6:11 "Give us today our daily bread."

Just as I carefully prepared for the lovely, shiny new lino-leum flooring by perfectly preparing the subfloor, I prepare my life for the installation of God's will and purpose by laying a subfloor of faith. Faith is what gives our lives and hopes substance. Faith is the undeniable evidence proving the hope of what we don't see yet as reality. Faith apprehends the reality of our prayers, it grasps the unseen desires of our hearts, and assures us with absolute certainty that God has heard and will answer our prayers.[4] Faith is what supports and keeps the beauty of our lives showing for years.

### The Preparation of Faith Takes Place Long Before the Leap of Faith.

When we look back at the foolishness of the first diver com-pared with the preparation of the second, two words can be used to describe the difference between them—*prepared* and *confident.*

Successful crossroads navigators know those two words intimately. They live in prepared confidence. Not just learning by experience, but being ready for those times when they have no experience—through preparation. Trusting God because they have spent time with Him and have watched Him work with others. They have learned to sense when He says the time is right, the conditions are favorable, and the leap of faith is appropriate. In other words, their faith has been prepared by relating closely to Him on a daily basis. It's a walk of faith, a lifestyle of faith.

Successful crossroads navigators are not foolish, high-tower "faith" divers. They have accepted the responsibility for showing up for training. For listening to the "Coach" and inching up the tower a little higher each day under His watch-ful eye and careful supervision. And furthermore, when the time is right for the dive, no one else can take it for them. They are the ones who've prepared, who've practiced, and who will climb the tower. Their teammates look on and encourage them, but the dive is theirs alone.

How about you? Have you foolishly climbed a tower too high for your preparation simply because you have seen oth-ers do it? If so, it's not too late. There's more than one way to

---

[4]Hebrews 11:1: "Now faith is being sure of what we hope for and certain of what we do not see."

descend from that dangerously high place. You don't have to jump just yet, you can climb back down the ladder. God will never condemn you for staying within your level of faith.

You'll get your chance to dive from the top—when He says you're prepared and ready. And when you do, it will be breathtaking and perfect. Because you see, high-tower divers don't begin on the tower or even in the pool below, they begin on the ground. And what's more, they're made from the inside out—from the heart. They don't climb the high tower to discover confidence for the next dive, they take it with them for this one.

If you become a successful crossroads navigator, it will be because you have purposed to manage your own faith. And you will have the wisdom to take those bold steps of faith only when you've been prepared and when God says you're ready. You'll know when that is, because He will tell you. And when you do, you won't have shaky knees or feel dizzy from fear. You will have substance, a foundation for your confidence.

Successful crossroads navigators are not the daredevils of faith—they are the students of it. And so are you. How about it? Do you feel ready to inch up that tower just a little bit higher today?

# 21

# "Lifestyle of the Rich and Interdependently Healthy"

---

### Purpose #5
**Live in healthy interdependence with
other believers.**

---

"Living on the wall," as rock-climbers will tell you, is a
perpetual process of clipping and unclipping things in and
out of anchors. The simple task of handing a water jug to a
rock-climbing partner becomes complex and requires precise
and practiced cooperation.

"Gimme the water."

"Let me unclip it. Here you go."

"Thanks."

"Got it?"

"Got it." *Clip.*

With so much clipping and unclipping, it's easy to get confused and accidentally unclip the wrong thing. A haul bag, rope, or a sleeping bag accidentally unclipped can fall thousands of feet and bring the most exciting wall-climbing adventure to a premature end.

One climber remembers accidentally unclipping a rack of pitons[1] on a high climb in Zion Canyon, Arizona. "We decided to retreat," he said. Even though they had enough pitons to complete the ascent his partner wanted to go back down.

"I'm not worried about you unclipping the rack," his partner told him. "I am worried that you might unclip me."

A valid concern. Rock-climbers know that being able to have confidence and trust in your partner is just as important as having the right equipment.

The intense sport of rock-climbing offers a clear example of mutual dependence. Each team member depending entirely on the other while accepting the responsibility for being depended upon is what we call interdependence.

It is too easy to throw words around assuming that those around us understand what we're talking about. We speak about the need for interdependence between Christians quite freely, but do we understand it? Can we explain it? Can we teach it? Do we model it?

But, more to the point, do we believe and live it?

As Christians, we live on the "Big Wall" every day. It's called life. And we don't live there alone, we are in harness with other believers who are making the climb alongside us. We affect them, they affect us. Just like rock-climbers, we help or hinder each other. We are interdependent.

Interdependence exists whenever two or more people become interrelated because they are mutually committed to an interest, cause, or institution.

Marriage is an interdependent adventure. Families are interdependent. The staff of a small office or a board of directors of a large corporation work interdependently. A church is made up of its interdependent members.

When those involved in an interdependent relationship have as their basis and purpose for belonging together their personal acceptance of Jesus Christ, their interdependence be-

---

[1] Piton is a spike with an eye for a rope, driven into rock or ice to support a mountain climber.

comes what we refer to as Christian interdependence. But lest you think all interdependence is healthy, think again.

Let us take a little "aside" into the concept of interdependence. It is important that we leave our main train of thought for a while in order to make sure our point is clearly communicated.

So much is said these days about being *co-dependent* that many genuine acts of compassion are misunderstood and suspected as unhealthy. On the other hand, dependence can often be misdiagnosed as a simple spiritual malady that can be rectified through repentance or trying harder. Worse yet, independence is often mistaken for strength and courage—even admired. To help clear up the confusion, a closer look at these three concepts is needed.

## Independent People

We know them, they are those who come and go at will. Free as a bird, they breeze in and out of our Bible studies and Sunday school classes autonomous and unattached. Self-confident, they have been known to show up at congregational business meetings more often than prayer meetings. They seem to always have their personal agendas ready and answers and remedies readily available for every ill that the church suffers. They aren't afraid to speak up. And, when things don't go the way they think they ought to, they wash their hands of the rest of us. Then, self-willed and headstrong, they make their way to another church in the area.

## Dependent People

Helpless and afraid, they attach themselves to anyone who will make themselves available. Hanging on for dear life, they unquestioningly take whatever instruction is given, follow the leader to extremes, and defenselessly swallow the devil's ridiculous lies and accusations. They become puppets to cult leaders, slaves to abusive leadership, and cling hopelessly to those who would take advantage of them. Void of identity, they only believe they are important as long as someone continually tells them so.

Dependent people can live interdependently, and probably do, but not in a healthy way. Not if there is a co-dependent wandering around.

## Co-dependent People

These crisis-oriented reactionaries live obsessively plugged in to other people's needs. With identities based in being needed they often draw a group of helpless dependents around them for mutual, but never-getting-anywhere support. Their self-worth is not only found in meeting the desperate needs in the lives of others—it depends on it. All the while completely ignoring their own. No sacrifice is too big, no personal price is too high—if you are helpless, hopeless, and weak there is usually a co-dependent waiting to plug in to your need. Not, you understand, to help you meet your need, but to meet it for you, and sadly in the process meet a need of their own—their need to be needed.

Perhaps you have recognized people you know in the preceding definitions. You might even agree that our churches are pretty well made up of all three groups. However, we don't have to be stuck accommodating the independent, nor coddling the dependent. Neither do we have to maintain the self-destructive patterns of co-dependency. There is a fourth option—healthy interdependence.

Let's look again at the sport of rock-climbing as our model.[2]

*Dynamic Number One:*

Healthy interdependence doesn't just happen. It is the result of understanding intention and commitment.

We really do affect each other by our attitudes, our commitments, and our level of involvement. We are a team. We are joined together by bonds of love in Christ just as surely as climbers are tied together as they scale the majestic face of a rock. What each member does or doesn't do affects the entire team.

We are one people.[3] Though we come from a variety of ethnic or cultural heritages, in Christ we become one people.

---

[2]Climbing information based on *Climbing Big Walls*, Mike Strassman, ICS Books, Inc. Merriville, IN, 46410, 1990. Used by permission.
[3]This mystery is that through the gospel the Gentiles are heirs together with Israel, members together of one body, and sharers together in the promise of Christ Jesus. Ephesians 3:6

We are one body. As members of Christ's body, each having a different purpose and function, we move and accomplish the tasks of building His kingdom when we recognize and appreciate that we are one. Members together of one body.

We share one promise. The promise of Christ's return for His people is our promise. Together we share the hope and anticipate His return. He's coming again, and when He does, it will be the fulfillment of His promise to us.

Commitment to healthy interdependence means that those involved are willing to invest time, energy, and patience with one another as we develop interdependently healthy skills.

We don't become interdependently healthy without intention. It requires awareness of where we've been, an appreciation of where others have also been, and an acute desire to blend and merge together regardless of our personal histories, faults, or individual progress.

## Dynamic Number Two:

Healthy interdependence means creating a reciprocal atmosphere of acceptance and affirmation.

Letting me be me, and letting you be you is the simple fact of acceptance. It has nothing to do with performance, but personhood. Individuals can only validate one another when expectations are dropped, masks are allowed to fall, and each person is seen as valuable to the group.

When we accept ourselves and present ourselves to others in a way that they perceive as authentic we find acceptance. When I am weak I can admit it, when I am feeling scared or confused, I can say so because in a healthy interdependent atmosphere there's no fear of being labeled weak, scared, and confused. In other words, my identity and individual worth is not perceived as coming out of my circumstance—but within me.

And, acceptance is a two-way street. If we are ever to fully experience the warmth and depth of interdependence, we must receive others as genuine. You see, interdependence must be available to all, or it isn't really available at all.

## Dynamic Number Three:

Healthy interdependence is based on completion, not competition.

Rock-climbers recognize the importance of both the

*climber* and the *anchor*. It is understood that only one member of the team climbs at a time. The climber leads and sets the protection, securing the way for the next climber while the anchor watches. While the climber is working and making progress the anchor stays alert and aware, protecting the climber. Together they are climbing the solid rock, but advancing only one at a time. Once the climber has reached the intermediate goal, or the high point of the pitch, the anchor or belayer prepares to trade roles with the climber. Inch by inch, they work together. Trading roles, protecting each other by setting and cleaning protection as they go. Each carrying their share of the equipment needed to make the climb. Mutually harnessing their energy, pooling their skills, and sharing the moment of victory at the summit.

In the same way, healthy interdependence emerges when we serve Jesus Christ as members of one team. There can be no jealousy concerning position, place, or imagined privilege when we view our Christian brothers and sisters as fellow servants, not competitors.

*Dynamic Number Four:*

Healthy interdependence is that wonderful understanding that with all our differences, all our varying strengths and weaknesses, none of us stand a chance alone—we really do need each other.

In his book, *Climbing the Big Walls*, Mike Strassman says it is one thing to climb a big wall with a partner, and it is altogether another thing to solo a big wall. The task of leading, rappelling, cleaning, and hauling each pitch combine to make soloing a big wall about three times as much effort and immeasurably more dangerous than with a partner.

There are no reprieves from the constant work of climbing when soloing. There are no rests while the partner climbs. The solo climber carries the entire responsibility for his safety, equipment, and progress alone. Keeping the rope out of the cracks where it can get stuck is a constant job. Strong winds pose a particular threat without a partner to belay. There's no room for error, no margin for safety when going it alone. One solo climber recalls a mishap.

"Once I inadvertently tied both ends of my lead line into the anchors. I came to the middle of the rope, twenty feet from the top before I realized I had both ends tied in and I was stuck." Thirty minutes later and countless calories burned in wasted energy, the climber resolved to be more careful.

Another climber reports, "I thought I had pulled down all the lead line slack. I had jumped to the lip of the last pitch of my climb when *whooooosh!*—I felt myself falling through the air. Unknowingly there had been almost 40 feet of lead line slack on top. The rope had wedged somehow near the top. Miraculously, I only fell 20 feet before the rope caught again . . . I was totally shaken up, I tell you."

It's the same for solo-Christians. No room for error, no love to cover faults and shortcomings. No one to remind them of God's grace and sufficiency, no one to know when they need help.

The work of soloing as a Christian isn't impossible, but it is about three times as much effort and immeasurably more dangerous than with a partner.

There are no reprieves from the constant effort required when soloing. There are no rests like there are when walking in healthy interdependence. The solo-Christian carries the entire responsibility for his safety, equipment, and progress all alone. Keeping himself out of difficulties and danger is a constant job. Without a partner to help, the solo-Christian walks a fine line. There's no room for error, no net of safety. No wonder Paul encouraged the early Christians to watch out for each other.

"Just as each of us has one body with many members, and these members do not all have the same function, so in Christ we who are many form one body, and each member belongs to all the others. Be devoted to one another in brotherly love. Honor one another above yourselves. Live in harmony with one another. Do not be proud, but be willing to associate with people of low position. Do not be conceited. If it is possible, as far as it depends on you, live at peace with everyone."[4]

Interdependence is our lifeline. It is the very thing that helps us successfully navigate our crossroads experiences in the safety and wisdom of other believers.

When an *independent* person comes to a crossroads, he often approaches it as a running back headed for the goal line. "Hey, wait," a teammate may call out.

---

[4]Romans 12:4–5, 10, 16, 18

"Wait, nothing! I'm going for it alone!" the independent insists.

When a *dependent* person is facing a crossroads, he'll probably bring the situation to his group or friends. "What are my options? What shall I do?" he says. "Can't someone please tell me what to do?"

When a *co-dependent* faces a decision, he comes to his friends and says, "What do you guys want me to do? How do you feel about this?" Though he may honestly sense he should make a different decision, if it would make someone unhappy or even run the risk of it, he will bury his own good judgment in favor of pleasing his friends.

But when a healthy *interdependent* is challenged to make a choice he brings the whole issue and its options to the group, lays it all out as best he can, and says, "I'd like your opinion. I know you can't make my decision for me, but I really value your insight and input before I make my decision. Please tell me if you think I have overlooked anything." He's really asking for it, you say? Yes, he is. But what if his group has taken as their model of relationship the following verses?

"Therefore each of you must put off falsehood and speak truthfully to his neighbor, for we are all members of one body."[5]

And,

"Do not lie to each other, since you have taken off your old self with its practices and have put on the new self, which is being renewed in knowledge in the image of its Creator."[6]

Asking for it? Let's all ask for it. Let us live the life of the interdependently healthy—lifestyles of the rich beyond measure. Let us find in interdependence the sense of worth and value we all long for. Not in hanging on to each other, but in holding each other up. An interconnected people, living linked in a healthy, safe way, knowing we are bonded eternally together because of Jesus.

One people, one body, one promise. Come here, I want to take your hand. We belong interdependently together.

[5]Ephesians 4:25
[6]Colossians 3:9–10

# 22

# Something Real

Several years ago, I (Zane) had a hunger for God and a desire to be used by Him that was so deep it gnawed at my heart day and night. I had made myself available, had studied and prepared myself for ministry, yet there was something deep within that didn't seem to be satisfied. An unspecific need, to be sure, but very real.

Attending a conference at Pastor Jack Hayford's Church on the Way in Southern California, I listened to every speaker intently. Enjoying the conference, I sang every song enthusiastically and praised God wholeheartedly. But quite unexpectedly, during a simple question-and-answer session with Pastor Jack, God spoke powerfully to my heart about my deep desire and indescribable need.

Someone in the back of the room stood and asked, "Pastor Jack, could you outline the number of hours you pray and study and share with us the key to your success?" I got ready to write. I wanted to make sure I would be able to remember the answer this great pastor was about to give.

Pastor Jack smiled and stuck his hands in his pockets. Quietly he stood looking over the group of pastors sitting in the very room and seats occupied week after week with the congregation of the Church on the Way. He waited before giving his answer.

"The test of this, of any ministry, is not in what you do— but in what you are. And," he continued, "if there is a key, it's wrapped up in this one phrase: integrity of heart. That you are always honest before God and before people."

Now, you understand, this was not a regular service, it had not been preceded with music and there was no organ-playing atmosphere during his answer. It was shop-talk among pastors. But never before had there been an insight that impacted me so deeply. That was it! That was my deepest desire, integrity! Complete honesty before men and before people.

That simple statement completely changed my ministry. Not that I had been less than honest before God and people as far as I knew. But from that day I *purposed* to be a man of integrity, of complete honesty before God and before people.

It's so easy to become enamored with the externals. Style, gifts, and charisma have been so over-emphasized that we are a generation of Christians that seem to be perfectly wired, having it all together, and sailing successfully unhindered through life. Surface Christians, just skimming along on the top by learning to say the right things, do the right things, and look the right way. Slogans and Christian terms roll easily off the tongue. Playing the part of the Christian is perceived to be the real Christian experience. *Lookin' good,* we say, while we're just barely getting by.

We seek after spiritual excitement but avoid experiences that would develop substance and character within us.

Have we forgotten that God is looking for faithfulness, uprightness, and integrity? Do we care?

Are we still aware that as God looked into the heart of David, he looks within ours as well? And what does He find there? Integrity? Honesty?

I am so convinced that the strength of our families and churches will not be because we "move in the gifts," but because we walk in integrity.

So much effort is being given today to finding and developing wholeness. But, lest we forget, wholeness isn't complete without integrity. Healing without purposing to be a person of integrity only leaves us open for more hurt and injury.

Integrity doesn't mean that we never make mistakes, nor does it mean that we're instantly perfect. It simply means that in all my mistakes, I purpose to remain honest before God.

It reminds me (Neva) of a time when I was heartbroken because my relationship with my daughter Sandra was shattered. I felt my whole life was collapsing, my family was fractured, and I was beside myself with deep pain.

In addition, like more than half of all adult American women, I was struggling with my weight. For me, though, it was different. I was the author of a million-copy Christian best seller on weight loss! And, if that wasn't enough, my father was dying. That's when my profound moment of "integrity" insight came.

All alone in my living room, long after midnight, I sobbed out my pain to God. Then in the quietness I simply turned to Psalm 23 for comfort and for some reason continued reading. The words of Psalm 26 penetrated my heart and spirit.

"Vindicate me, O LORD, for I have led a blameless life; I have trusted in the LORD without wavering. Test me, O LORD, and try me, examine my heart and my mind; for your love is ever before me, and I walk continually in your truth."[1]

*Integrity.* Never before has a reminder about integrity been needed as much as it is now. Our entire nation is threatened at this very moment with the potential for destruction because of compromise and lack of integrity in business, in churches, and in our government.

Our leaders appear to be square-shooting, decent, and moral. But the reality of corruption and deceit is ever present. Where is integrity? Are words like honesty, uprightness, and faithfulness lost to us forever? Has truthfulness and trustworthiness been banned like prayer in the public schools?

High government officials tell blatant untruths. Sometimes they use artful distortions that are technically true but misleading. And the effect? The destruction of public trust in leaders and eventually in our whole political system. All because of a lack of integrity.

And it's all too true at home. Exaggerations, simplifica-

---

[1] Psalm 26:1–3.

tions, and over-promises show lack of integrity. Half truths create incredibility factors and credibility gaps.

A lack of integrity compiles one incident upon another until the impression is finally formed of people who are forever trying to explain themselves. Perhaps even incapable of facing and telling the unvarnished truth. Lack of integrity forces people to talk their way around almost any inconsistency. Saying one thing and doing another.

We all understand that a person can make mistakes and still recover. But once integrity is lost and reputation is damaged, it is hard to retrieve. Hard, but not impossible. And it happens in the heart—an open, honest heart before God.

## God Walks With You

There are three important things God does for those who walk with a heart of integrity.

*First, He warns the person of integrity when a mistake is about to be made.*

In Genesis, chapter twenty, we read that a king named Abimelech sent for Sarah. He wanted to have her as his wife. He had been told that Sarah was Abraham's sister—technically true, she was his stepsister. But Sarah was more than Abraham's sister, she was his wife. She wasn't available for marriage. God didn't mince words with Abimelech, "You touch her, and you're a dead man!"

Wait a minute, Sarah had been passed off as Abraham's sister. According to the culture, Abimelech had done nothing wrong. But he was a man of integrity. Had he known, he wouldn't have even cast a second glance in her direction. If he had taken her and it had come out later that she was a married woman and the king had taken her for himself, he would have been guilty of adultery.

"She's married," God said.

"Hey, I didn't know!" Abimelech responded.

"I know that," God said. "That's why I'm telling you now—so you won't make a mistake."

What a powerful principle. If we are moving with a heart that is right before God, it opens the way for God to warn us from taking a step that would prove to be destructive.

We're all just human. We are limited in our knowledge and we can make decisions and do things that could be damaging to our lives. But when we walk with integrity of heart before God, we can expect God to warn us—to help us before we make a fatal mistake. Now, we also understand that is no guarantee we will listen to His warning. If we were completely open with one another, most of us would have to admit to ignoring Him—even when the warning lights have flashed wildly within our hearts and minds.

It is also no guarantee that we won't from time to time make mistakes or do really dumb things because we didn't recognize God's warning.

*Second, integrity gives God a reason to defend us when we can't defend ourselves.*

In Psalm twenty-five, David, finding himself surrounded by the enemy, realizes the forces coming at him from every side are too much for him. He admits his resources are not adequate and that without God's intervention all he has received from God's hand will be ripped off.

His prayer is one of honest appeal on the basis of his integrity. "Come to my aid," David asks. "Become my defender."

That's what happened to me (Neva) as I struggled with my credibility as a mother. In quietness I found strength, and God became my defender. Was I a perfect mother? Hardly. Did God deal with the mistakes I made with Sandy? Certainly. Did God come to my assistance and defense. More than once. And was my relationship with Sandy ever restored—thankfully, yes.

*Third, integrity gives God the go-ahead to perpetuate His kingdom through us.*

In 1 Kings, chapter nine, we find God speaking to Solomon, "As for you, if you walk before me in integrity of heart and uprightness, as David your father did, and do all I command and observe my decrees and laws, I will establish your royal throne over Israel forever, as I promised David your father when I said, 'You shall never fail to have a man on the throne of Israel.' "

Sadly, Solomon didn't walk in integrity of heart, and his reign that began in a blaze of glory ended tragically. Why? Because he compromised, little by little his kingdom began to weaken. A lack of integrity brought to an early end that which God desired to perpetuate forever.

Everyone of us can probably remember seeing repeatedly the national tragedy of January 28, 1986. At 11:39 A.M., Eastern Standard Time, barely a minute after a successful lift-off, we watched in stunned disbelief the explosion that sent the crew of the Challenger to their deaths. How could this have happened? What went wrong?

In a television interview, a former commander revealed the incredible truth. "Just before the explosion, the craft was experiencing maximum dynamic pressure. Yet it was built to withstand that pressure. Somewhere the integrity of the craft was violated and compromised, therefore leaving it vulnerable. The key to the success of any mission is the integrity of the spacecraft. Even though it was constantly checked and rechecked to make sure that the integrity was maintained, somewhere that integrity was compromised."

It's a memory and a lesson we should never forget. When those maximum points of pressure come—and they will—there can be no compromise of our integrity.

History has shown us clearly what happens in the lives of Christians and even among Christian leadership when integrity is compromised.

## Tested and Trusted

How can we walk in integrity? Very simple. Psalm 26 says, "I have trusted in the Lord. . . ." That's where it begins. We can't make integrity, we can't grow it. It's nothing we can do in our own strength, wisdom, or knowledge. We can't educate ourselves into integrity nor rely on our own judgment or abilities. Simply trusting in the Lord, we open our hearts to His inspection and examination.

"Test me, O LORD, and try me, examine my heart and my mind. . . ." No closed-off areas where God is refused access is how we come into and maintain integrity. Letting every situation in our lives be used by God can strengthen and prove our integrity.

Looking into your heart, would God see that you are totally His? Is He given total control of your life?

"For your love is ever before me, and I walk continually in your truth." Integrity doesn't mean you will live forever perfect and flawless. But it does mean that when God's love is our focus, our hope, and given our main attention, we face struggles and personal pressure points with integrity. When we make mistakes, we correct them with integrity. When we do wrong, with integrity we repent. And when we suffer? We do well to preserve our integrity so that our suffering profits us through added understanding, deepened compassion, and increased faith.

When His love is ever before us, we can meditate on Him instead of mull over our shortcomings. And when we walk in truth we accept what He, not others, says about us. When we cling to His word it assures us that our position and identity in Christ are secure—no matter how awful we may feel about ourselves.

Proverbs 4:20–23 tells us to watch over our hearts. In other words, to guard our integrity. Our marriages, our business and social relationships, and the people we worship with all depend on our integrity before the Lord.

Successful crossroads navigators know that some of the choices they will face will cause major stress and pressure points. That's no time to be checking for integrity of heart. Integrity must be maintained.

So how is it with you when no one is looking? Are you willing to come to terms with and not cover up secret sin, and repent, even if no one could ever find out about it? Are you willing to come clean before God, honestly walking in integrity—not willing to "just get by"?

Integrity, so essential to our success, is really very simple. It is simply living our lives in front of Jesus. Keeping His truth, welcoming His Word as the lamp unto our feet and the light unto our pathway, and choosing to never let that light be put out.

Think of it this way, you may be able to navigate a crossroads once, maybe even twice without integrity, but you will never become a successful crossroads navigator without it.

# 23

# Taking the Path of the Most Resistance

---

### Purpose #7

**Become persevering—and you will become an overcomer.**

---

He was a rather masculine-looking man, shopping in a fabric store. It seemed as though he knew what he was doing, that he had been in the store before. It soon became obvious that he wasn't there with his wife, but walked directly toward some of the brightest neon-orange nylon I had ever seen. The writer in me (Neva) gave me a push of curiosity and I moved toward him. I waited for the opportunity and then asked my simple question.

"Excuse me, sir," I said.

"Yes?" He looked up from the fabric bolt.

"I don't mean to be nosy"—although I really did—"but what are you going to do with that material?"

"I'm making parachutes." He smiled at me and then continued, "I'm a sprint coach. I make small parachutes, attach them to flag football belts, and my sprinters wear them during practice. It's called resistance training."

"Resistance training?" I had no idea what he meant.

"Resistance training means making it harder for the sprinters in practice so that when they run in the real event they have a better edge—you know, over the competition."

"Is that right?"

"There are other kinds of resistance training, too. We make our runners run through sand, over uneven terrain, and uphill as much as possible. When they get really in shape, we make them wear the parachute while they run uphill in sand!" He laughed. "Our sprinters think we're trying to kill them. But when they meet the competition, then they are glad we've been hard on them in training."

"Do you have a winning team?"

"Well, that depends."

"On the competition?"

"No, on the team." He gathered his bolt of fabric and turned to leave. "If they make it through the training, they're already winners. It doesn't matter what the competition does then. Because winning doesn't happen on the track, it happens up here." He pointed at his temple.

It clicked with something I had heard years ago. Serious marathon runners train at high altitudes for one simple reason—it's harder to run at high altitudes. Once they adapt to the altitude, they keep adding weights to their wrists, waists, and even ankles, in preparation for the big race. "It's as if I have an extra pair of legs when I come down from the mountain to the race," one runner said.

"Let us not become weary in doing good, for at the proper time we will reap a harvest if we do not give up" (Galatians 6:9).

This training concept gives new insight to Hebrews 12:1: "Therefore, since we are surrounded by such a great cloud of witnesses, let us throw off everything that hinders and the sin that so easily entangles, and let us run with perseverance the race marked out for us."

Mostly, we think of entering the race unencumbered by sins, but it is more. You see, while the training requires the extra weights, the race is hindered by them. In other words, endurance in the race depends on perseverance in training. When the race is run, the weights are left at the training sight, not worn on the track.

Life is hard. We wish we could say it were easier, but it's not. What's more, the Christian life is harder. Not such good news for those who can barely keep their heads above water or who feel like they've recently been thrown a curve. But that's just part of the story.

Though the Christian life is harder, it has meaning and purpose. And it has power and hope.

God calls us to have faith. Yet, right here in His own Word, He promises us not only faith but the testing of it. And for good reason. I'm sure you agree that if our faith was never tested, we'd get stronger all right, but would we have strength?

If your faith has been hanging by a single gossamer thread and you see that one or two of the strands are beginning to fray, don't despair. Before you go off the deep end, realize that the enemy will send out little feelers to see if you are ready to throw in the towel. If not, he'll try to plant a doubt or two, maybe try to lead you down the garden path emotionally or mentally, trying to make you wonder if you're lost. When that happens, remember the little emergency broadcast signal and let it sound throughout your mind—"BEEEEEEEEEP! This is only a test. If it had been a real emergency, you would have been given instructions as to what to do."

## Meeting the Challenge!

Circumstances don't line up with what you know God has called you to do. Money is tight, the timing isn't right. Somehow, it seems that even though it was going along all right yesterday, today a monkey wrench has been thrown into the works. The best laid plans have gone sour. Now what?

It's challenge time. Problems arise, barriers come from the strangest places, and more questions remain than answers. Riding on the horns of a dilemma is not the way you expected to travel, but here you are. If circumstances don't change, well, it looks like it's all down the tubes. Right? Maybe not. Perhaps there's more. Instead of brooding over impending doom, take a look beyond at the opportunity that's just around the corner—if you can get around the corner.

## The Promise Contest!

Our enemy, the devil, has been contesting God's will from the very beginning. If he were to be in a court of law every time he wanted to lodge a protest against what God has promised His children, he would be thrown out as a nuisance. He is so persistent in his efforts that it can be tempting to give in rather than go on. But wait! If he were able to throw God's promises overboard, wouldn't he have succeeded by now? History itself proves that he's playing a losing hand! *Don't give up yet.* God's promises are secure, maybe even more secure because they are being contested.

## Perseverance Is Not the Same As Endurance

Hanging on, hanging tough, and holding the line is not perseverance, it's endurance. Often we think we are persevering but can't understand our lack of progress. Whenever you simply ride it out, buckle up, and hang on until help comes, you have endured. But, before you condemn yourself, there are times when that's all that's possible or appropriate. Endurance is where your faith is built, and it keeps your faith intact. It would be foolish to expect or attempt any more. Other times, it is appropriate to do more than just see it through or stick it out.

There are those times when it is appropriate to get on your grubby clothes, pick up your tools and plug away. More than going the distance, or holding your ground, perseverance is making something of the situation. Perseverance is going the distance, making it to the end, plus going beyond the possibilities, jumping the hurdles, and climbing the obstacles.

Romans 5:1–5 outlines the perseverance process: "Therefore, since we have been (1) justified through faith, (2) we have peace with God through our Lord Jesus Christ, through whom we have gained access by faith into this grace in which we now stand. And (3) we rejoice in the hope of the glory of God. Not only so, but we also rejoice in our sufferings, because (4) we know that suffering produces perseverance; (5) perseverance, character; and (6) character, hope. And hope does not disappoint us, because God has poured out His love into our hearts by the Holy Spirit, whom He has given us."

We are not crazy. We are hopeful. We have not lost our senses. We have come to a better way of dealing with life than merely coping, we have purposed to persevere!

"His divine power has given us everything we need for life and godliness through our knowledge of Him who called us by His own glory and goodness. Through these He has given us His very great and precious promises, so that through them you may participate in the divine nature and escape the corruption in the world caused by evil desires. For this very reason, make every effort to add to your faith goodness; and to goodness, knowledge; and to knowledge, self-control; and to self-control, perseverance; and to perseverance, godliness; and to godliness, brotherly kindness; and to brotherly kindness, love. For if you possess these qualities in increasing measure, they will keep you from being ineffective and unproductive in your knowledge of our Lord Jesus Christ" (2 Peter 1:3–8).

## Perseverance Is Faith in Action!

So often we think exercising our faith is the same as running the race. But tell me, does it make sense for a runner to wait to exercise his muscles until he meets the competition on the track? No, of course not. In the same way, faith is exercised, being strengthened for the real event in perseverance. Look at it this way, endurance is when we hold our faith, perseverance is when we exercise our faith, and the race is when we put our faith to the test.

In other words, perseverance isn't the goal, it's a key part of the training process. Winning the race is the goal.

## Overcoming Is the Main Event

This chapter has pretty much described a growth process— a process through which our faith grows and we mature as Christians. And for good reason. We have been destined to become overcomers. Without the lessons of endurance and perseverance, overcoming would not be possible.

Overcomers are not the super-heroes or the caped crusaders of the Christian world. They are the plain, ordinary people, living regular lives but who have purposed to become trained overcomers through perseverance.

Overcomers cannot become overcomers without obstacles to overcome. Just like life is stress and stress is life. Just like prayer is faith and faith is prayer. Overcomers face obstacles and obstacles face overcomers. Can you become a mountain climber without the mountain? Can you become a sailor without the wind?

Overcomers have learned to plan for obstacles by persevering in the training sessions. In other words, persevering while jumping smaller obstacles prepares them for larger obstacles.

Overcomers have learned to expect obstacles that are unplanned for, unexpected, and unknown. Or, they have learned to prepare for the worst, while expecting and hoping for the best.

Overcomers are those right around us who have developed a strategy for success. They persevere. In their quiet times, in prayer, in worship, in service. They persevere in maintaining their spiritual health and their faith and they persevere in integrity. Simply stated, overcomers have purposed to mature.

Overcomers know to turn to God's Word for hope. They know how to turn in healthy interdependence to other believers for support and encouragement.

Overcomers know by heart the meaning of the words, "I have fought the good fight, I have finished the course, I have kept the faith." Because as perseverers they have learned to say, "I am fighting the good fight, I am finishing the course, I am keeping the faith."

Successful crossroads navigators only make it *look* easy when they face the challenges of their crossroads. But so do world-class skiers and professional basketball players. Persevering is much harder work than overcoming. But remember this, overcoming will be impossible if we haven't first purposed to persevere.

And successful crossroads navigators do more than just purpose—they fill their hearts and lives with principles. In the final section of this book we will look closely at those principles and show you how you can become principled, too.

# *Part Four*

## Successful Crossroads Navigators Live Principled Lives

It may seem that, with all the work done in the first three sections of this book, decisions and crossroads navigation should be easy. After all, a person who knows all the secrets, made the choices necessary to re-order their inner life, and targets their life with purpose, is ready for anything. Right? Hardly. Such a position can be deadly and even undo all the hard work that has gone on so far. Deadly, that is, unless certain principles are in place and functioning.

Each of us lives with certain principles already in place.

Take for example a group of pedestrians waiting to cross an intersection downtown in any major metropolitan area. The pedestrians' crossing signal has just turned from "walk" to a flashing "don't walk." Some will stop, obediently waiting on the sidewalk until the light changes to the green "walk" signal again. Others will quicken their steps to make it through the cross-walk before the traffic light turns yellow. Still others ignore the signal light completely and dodge oncoming cars and provoke the drivers. Each pedestrian is operating by his own set of principles concerning traffic laws and signals. In the same way, we operate by an individual set of principles when facing a crossroads experience. Choices have to be made, sometimes on the spot or within certain time constraints, and though we may appear to respond instinctively, we are really acting on our principles.

Unfortunately, our principles may be mistakenly based on personal prejudice or past experience. Neither of which prepare stretching, growing Christians adequately for future decisions that require trust and faith to navigate uncharted territory. Our crossroads choices are far more risky than crossing a busy intersection and should be perceived as such. Our crossroads choices affect all future crossroads choices and often determine whether or not we are in the right place, at the right time, for God's will to be advanced in our lives. Crossroads choices are so important, in fact, they must be faced with sound biblical principles operating within us, not just instinctive or experiential ones.

Successful crossroads navigators know they cannot live on inner direction alone. Principles based on external signals and how circumstances are viewed and handled are often the key between success and failure. They know that to live unprincipled is to live *presumptuously*. And that is dangerous indeed.

Wisdom tells even the most successful crossroads navigator that life cannot be reduced to a formula approach. What worked one time may be a stumbling block the next. God continually stretches His children. Serving Him wholeheartedly only means life gets more challenging, not less.

This fourth and final section presents several key principles that crossroads navigators find essential to successful decision-making and crossroads navigating.

# 24

# Making Optional Plans— Not Taking Detours

---

## Crossroads Principle #1

### Consider all the options.

---

Crossroads choices must be made with care because cross-roads are critical. They are those milestone moments that need to be handled with care and courage. Every successful crossroads navigator knows what the words "the heart is deceitful above all things"[1] mean, especially when decision time approaches. Though we have laid the foundations of our faith very carefully and put our hopes in God alone, the heart can still lead us away from God's best when we are presented with choices. Because we are aware of the weakness within the human personality, considering every option is a principle we cannot afford to overlook or avoid.

We are not talking about the relatively simple choices of

---

[1]Jeremiah 17:9

choosing the right color and make of car we will drive. We consider such things as cost, reputation, and features. We look for the best financing, and whether the car will serve our needs, get good gas mileage, and so on. We may even ask our friends how they like their cars and consult the most recent *Consumer Reports* for information and guidance. However, most of our crossroads choices are *much more critical* in nature.

Going to this college or that university isn't a simple choice. It means making lifelong connections and networking that will be important to our careers long after we turn the tassels at graduation.

Free-lancers and entrepreneurs know what it's like to wonder: "Should I keep my day job, or take the risk of a full-time business of my own?" Choosing to take the job here or accepting the position across the country affects not only our lives and causes us to adjust to a new town or church, but the lives of our family members are also affected. Relocation may determine who our children will meet and marry.

Whether we choose public schools or Christian education for our kids isn't the same as choosing a carpet for the house. It's a much more important matter, requiring careful consideration and intense prayer. It is a deeply personal decision and either choice might be met with criticism and misunderstanding.

Comparing such important life-changing options is often more difficult because it includes taking greater risks and the choice has a much broader impact. These options have to be considered in light of family, the future, God's leading, and whatever personal sacrifice is required.

There are also other even more crucial crossroads choices to be made. Crossroads which present options that are not just choices between tangibles, but intangibles. Who hasn't struggled with choosing between anger and forgiveness? Or bitterness or freedom from the past? Trust or fear?

Most of us have experienced coming to a crossroads of hope or doubt, of having to choose obedience or self-gratification. And haven't we all come to an intersection marked security and insecurity?

Growth through risk or stagnation by playing it safe is still just as scary for some as ever. Many, not wanting to consider each option, still prefer leaving it to chance over having to make a choice. Such options are often quite difficult to admit and explore. When crossroads experiences require us to think about the abstract, take paths unseen or unknown, or require a similar yet really quite different approach to our decisions, they present an inner personal challenge—the challenge of choice. A challenge many would like to avoid if possible.

Many would rather not have to consider all the options. Stuck in self-destructive patterns of laziness they opt to take the easy way out, the route of least resistance is just too tempting. "Thinking is too hard," they complain, "considering options takes too long, makes me work at decision time." Preferring to coast rather than consider, to drift than decide.

Others avoid option-consideration out of fear—I might have to stretch and grow, or worse, change. I might have to make a decision rather than be a victim of circumstance. And, horror of horrors, I might make a mistake! Some cannot conquer the fear of failure, or face the fact they might have to say "I'm sorry" later. They can't live with the possibility that they might have to admit they could be wrong or be embarrassed. They might have to admit they didn't have it all together, and so find it easier to let the decision make itself. Then they can say the results are not their fault. Fear also keeps some from choosing to consider the options because they might have to face the realities (or perhaps even pain) that option consideration sometimes forces. Then the truth of how things are is too threatening in light of how things can be, or worse yet, of how things should be.

Fear fosters a *pre-set* mind—which amounts to something like stubbornness. This is not the same as the made-up mind we'll talk about in a later chapter. Pre-set minds say by their unwillingness to look at options, "If I look at the options, I may not get what I want. I may have to change my mind, opinion, or direction. I can't look like I didn't have all the facts or that I didn't know all there was to know. I might look foolish. I'll just pretend my way through this decision and blame others for its less than desirable outcome if it all goes sour."

And, there are those who are simply overwhelmed by choices. Decisions are difficult enough, let alone the many options our decisions present. Overwhelmed, they really may be saying, "I don't know how to consider options, the whole process is confusing to me."

## Considering Options Is Not an Option

Though considering options is a lot of hard work, there are undeniable reasons that options must be considered. Let's list some of them.

*1. Considering options is how we learn the ways of God.* Looking at every situation from every conceivable angle and approach helps each option come into clearer focus. We see which options cancel others out, which are impossible, which are improbable, and which really are options, even if they are blocked by an obstacle.

*2. Considering options helps us grow and become responsible.* Thinking things through is not a waste of time, but a valuable way to redeem it. It has been said, "While there may not be time to do things right, there is always time to do it over." Good use of our God-given time is to use it wisely and carefully. Consideration of options helps us to do it right the first time.

*3. Considering options is one of the ways we experience God's testing—and it's a way we prove Him.* We can never see as clearly the hidden malice in our hearts as when God leads us to a crossroads experience that requires we be totally benevolent. We can only prove Him when we have submitted to His testing of us.

I (Zane) could have never known how able God was to provide for our congregation had I not proven Him through a recent building program of our church. However, each option we had to consider, each decision and choice that had to be made, not only to begin the project but to finish it, tested me beyond what I thought possible. Proving God and God testing me seemed to go hand in hand. I could never have proven Him without submitting to His testing of me at the same time.

*4. Considering all the options is an opportunity to try our wings.* If we carefully consider each possible alternative, follow each lead to its end, we truly learn our abilities and discover the content of our character. It gives us experimental opportunities before we commit to the point of no return.

*5. Considering all the options helps us mature.* It is where our childishness is called on the carpet and our adulthood takes center stage. It means we go from talking to walking our faith.

*6. Considering all the options gives us a chance to prove*

*we are serious about those things God considers serious.* I (Neva) have come to such a crossroads during the writing of this book. Without going into all the details, I'll just say that I've had a lifelong struggle with my identity as a writer. Twenty-five-plus titles has not helped me with this identity crisis as much as considering alternative careers. But recently the Lord made it clear that this is no longer to be an unsettled issue. He not only called me to be a writer, *He calls me a writer.* Period. The only options I am to consider from here on is what kind of writing I'll do. I have explored all the other job options. Getting a secretarial job is out—I need one of my own just to keep me on-track! Going back into retail management isn't for me, either. I'm not suited for the hotel business and I know I couldn't survive on an assembly line. Since I'm too young to retire and really do enjoy writing anyway, it's pretty clear—God takes me seriously as a writer and wants me take it seriously as well.

Considering all the options can be threatening, overwhelming, and confusing. But when we become principled people we discover the way it's done:

*1. Pause—Pray.* Option consideration is a personal responsibility; no one else can do the hard work of option consideration for you. Therefore, making options a matter of prayer makes sense. It gives God a chance to speak to you about the options and time to speak into the situation. It may seem strange that the first step to making wise decisions is to wait, but it is a purposeful delay—it is a thinking, praying delay.

*2. Differentiate between an option and a mandate.* Not every opportunity is a calling. When we know what God has called us to be and do, each option takes on new meaning and serves a good purpose. Not every option is a simple choice between right and wrong. Most are only degrees of difference between good, better, and best. When you know what God's calling is, you can more readily see that even good can stand in the way of having His best. That something appearing to be better isn't always better. For example, when we know that God has mandated us to evangelize the world, settling for less of this world's goods and comforts isn't sacrifice, it's the blessing of service.

*3. Do your homework.* Getting all the facts means much more than just listing all the positive/negatives. It also means being able to anticipate the impact the possible choices will have on your family. Getting all the facts is a way to step into objectivity, to outline a plan and predict obstacles and challenges.

*4. See options in light of God's known will—the big picture.* Know your priorities. Understand the importance of balance and seek to integrate all aspects of your life. Work, rest, and recreation are just as important to a healthy, balanced, and productive life as responsibilities and ministry.

*5. Seek counsel.* Nothing can take the place of the counsel of God's Word, of course. But to think we don't need counsel in addition to it is foolishness.

God gave us elders, pastors, and other mature Christians to help us consider our options. We can also have the benefit of our peers, especially if those relationships are what we could call covenant relationships. Covenant relationships are healthy relationships that include accountability and give others the freedom to speak truthfully to us. We can greatly benefit from different perspectives and the opportunity to think about other options and consider ideas we may have overlooked.

Counsel can protect us. "This is what I see" often means there can be more to our situation than our closeness allows us to see. Accountability helps us avoid "doing our own thing" and helps us share the risk.

When seeking counsel a few important safeguards would be wise to remember. First, seek those who will speak the truth, even if it's in conflict with you and your point of view. Second, don't stack the deck. In other words, tell your counselor or counselors all, not just select information. Third, guard against over-dependence on their counsel. Remember, your decisions are your responsibility. Fourth, know the wisdom of many counselors. It won't be confusing; remember, differing perspectives is desired. Fifth, always take counsel to the Lord. Sixth, don't overlook God-given counselors such as spouse, children, and other family members. Finally, test counsel with God's Word and submit to the inner witness of the Holy Spirit. After spending time in counseling, spend time in God's presence.

*6. Test each option as if it were the decision itself.* In other words, try on the decision, seeing how it fits before buying the whole idea. Option consideration is a dress rehearsal for our choices. It's where we work the bugs out of our plans.

And after you've carefully considered each option? This is only the beginning of a principled life. There are more principles to be put into place before we make the final choice or crossroads decision. Once we have narrowed the options, even considered one or two as possible finalists, it's time to move to the next principle—it's time to count the cost.

# 25

# Asking All the Tough Questions

---

## Crossroads Principle #2
### Count the cost.

---

Believe it or not, the same people who hesitate to consider options for fear they won't want what they get or get what they want hesitate to count the cost for many of the same reasons. The tough question "how much will this cost?" is often interpreted, "maybe I can't have it if I find out how much it costs." However, personal sacrifice will be made and the full price paid whether you count the cost or not.

If the sacrifice will still be made and the price fully paid, why then count the cost? Isn't it better not to know, rather than be discouraged or disheartened by the cost involved in our decisions?

No, it is never better not to know, and asking the tough questions is never easy. However, knowing what I am willing to personally invest or sacrifice to see my choice become reality is necessary and even beneficial to my personal growth and maturity. Counting the cost involves several simple yet difficult questions: Am I willing? Am I able? Is it possible? Is it probable? What will it take? How will I manage to get what it will take? What's more, no one else has the answers to these questions.

Not being willing to make those kinds of estimates and face the realities of counting the cost, some people resort to other tactics to get what they want.

They try to get what they want, to have their say in choice matters, by looking for ways to "creatively finance" their choice. For example, they may manipulate, scheme, or even pout, demanding that God (or those of us who live with them) give to them what they want while the rest of us pay for it. Living their dreams at our expense. But it doesn't work.

One night a cutting-edge type of guy approached Jesus.[1] "Teacher, what good thing must I do to get eternal life?" Jesus gave him a simple answer.

"Keep the commandments," He said.

"Which ones?" the young man asked.

"All of them," Jesus said.

"But I do that already. What else?"

"Go sell," Jesus answered, "sell your possessions and give to the poor, and you will have treasure in heaven. Then come, follow me."

But that was asking too much. The price was too high. He had too much stuff. Nobody else was asked to pay so much, why should he? Sorrowfully, the Bible says, he turned and went away.

Sadly, he didn't get the point.

You see, counting the cost is not the same as window shopping at the mall or sticker shopping new car lots on a Saturday afternoon. Counting the cost is simply coming to a place of being fairly firm about certain choices and decisions, knowing the price and then learning how to "arrange for the financing." We do that by asking the tough questions.

## How will my chosen option impact me financially?

Can I afford to take the risk? What adjustments might I have to make in my lifestyle? What will it mean to my giving and

---

[1] Matthew 19:16–30

186 / *Living By Chance or By Choice*

spending habits? What will I have to give up to follow this option to its completion or fulfillment?

What will the personal financial implications of my chosen option be? Am I willing to make those choices and adjustments?

On the other hand, can I afford not to take the risk? What will it cost me to remain secure and protected financially? I wonder what this rich young man of Matthew 19 would tell us now? Would he have done what Jesus asked if given the chance again?

### How will this option or choice impact my time?

Can I fit this decision and the time it will require if it becomes a reality into my already busy schedule? Or, what changes in my schedule will need to be made to accommodate my choice? Do I dare make such drastic changes? What happens if I don't? What would be the cost to me if I choose to keep my self-ordered calendar under my own control and preferences? If I don't have the time, will I make the time? If there isn't time, will I take the time?

### How will this option or choice impact me?

How will I be different if I put this option into place? What will I have to change? Am I willing to change if necessary?

### How will this option impact my friends and family?

Am I asking them to make a sacrifice or investment so that I get what I want or think is best? Is that okay? Is it appropriate?

A friend once took a job so demanding her family relationships and several friendships soon began suffering from neglect. "I'm sorry," she said. "But, I've got to do this for me right now. I don't know how long this will last, but I have to trust that when it's all said and done, my real and lasting relationships will still be there." Sadly, her real and lasting friendships aren't like securities or bonds you can stash away in a safe deposit box.

Maybe she counted the cost—maybe not. One friend said, "We all knew she would be sacrificing for this job. What we didn't know was she would sacrifice us."

Is it ever appropriate to ask family and friends to sacrifice for us and the decisions we feel we must make? Of course. If what we are doing has the potential to impact more than our personal interests, and once we're sure God is in charge—that we are truly responding to His voice and leading—we can boldly ask others to sacrifice and contribute. Our counselors can help us with this. God's voice and leading never violates the principles of His Word, and when we know without a doubt we are moving in those principles it is fitting that we be bold in asking others to make voluntary sacrifices alongside us. However, if the goal is based on personal or selfish agendas, we'd better think again. We are probably moving in presumption rather than principle.

Ask yourself the tough questions: What changes will my family have to make to accommodate this option or choice? How will my family change, how will life change if I ask my family to help make this option work? Am I willing to ask them? Are they willing to support me in this? Tough questions.

### How will this option impact my present responsibilities?

What will I have to finish before I can put this new plan into place? What responsibilities will I have to give up in order for this option to become operative? If this option were put into place right now, would I be forced to quit rather than finish out a responsibility? Is that appropriate? Would someone else have to pick up where I left off and finish my job? What sacrifice and adjustments would this decision force others to make? No easy answers here, either.

### How would this option or choice impact my personal involvement and ability to support others in places of responsibility and leadership?

Given the focus many of our choices demand, the energy they require and the attention they need, will my choosing a certain direction or option let someone down who depends on me? Will my already overloaded Christian Education director be forced to find a replacement in the middle of the term? What happens to the children and the continuity of their teaching? Will the choir director feel the impact of my withdrawal from the music program three days before Christmas? Will the pastor understand if I choose to support another ministry financially—in the middle of a missions-giving campaign?

You see, when we say yes, we also say no. Yes to a new decision, and no to one or more old ones. Something always gives when we take on something new. Counting the cost doesn't mean we never make a change, but that we fully understand the change and its impact and then find a way to help make the transition easier for all concerned.

*How can I choose this option without neglecting or ignoring other needs or issues?*

Taking on a new responsibility, making a new choice or going in a new direction can be exciting and wonderful. It offers us new enthusiasm and releases a whole flood of new ideas and creativity. However, there is a price to pay, a cost to count. We don't quit one thing to begin another. We finish—then we go on.

Just moving "to a new address" because it is exciting and motivating can serve to selfishly avoid dealing with deeper issues like perseverance or irresponsibility.

Remember, the question is not can I choose, but *how* can I choose this new option without neglecting other responsibilities? Let your creativity flow. You can find a way if you're willing to count the cost.

The Bible speaks of counting the cost. It shows us deeper meaning and even the purpose of such hard emotional work.

Sacrifice.

*Counting the cost helps us remember that sacrifice is not supposed to be a bargain.* David knew that. He sinned before God and God was about to punish the people for it. David pleaded with God to count the sin against him alone; the people were innocent. God said He would forgive the sin in response to a sacrifice offered in a certain place, in an exact way. David agreed and set out to meet God's terms. Approaching the owner of the field God specified, David said, "Sell it to me at the full price."

The Bible says[2] that the field owner said to David, "Take it! Let my lord the king do whatever pleases him. Look, I will give the oxen for the burnt offerings, the threshing sledges for the wood, and the wheat for the grain offering. I will give all this."

---

[2] 1 Chronicles 21:23

What a deal! Settling accounts with God, and at no cost to him! But David knew better.

But King David replied to Araunah, "No, I insist on paying the full price. I will not take for the LORD what is yours, or sacrifice a burnt offering that costs me nothing."

In other words, a sacrifice is supposed to cost you something. A bargain sacrifice is no sacrifice. David paid the full price and God honored David's integrity.

David built an altar to the Lord there and sacrificed burnt offerings and fellowship offerings. He called on the Lord, and the Lord answered him with fire from heaven on the altar of burnt offerings.

*Counting the cost means that though we pay nothing for salvation, we know it is not free.* You are not your own, the Bible says, you were bought with a price.[3] Jesus himself counted the cost for your eternal life. Furthermore, someone paid the price in prayer, gave sacrificially for the work of the kingdom, and stood in faith for your salvation experience. And most of us know that while we did not pay for our own way, we will be required to contribute for another's. Cost counters consider that as a normal part of the Christian life.

Cost counters accept a reciprocal form of responsibility and abandon the consumer mentality once and for all. The Christian life freely offers and we all are the grateful receivers. But it is more, it is also giving to those who could in no way ever benefit us in return.

*Counting the cost means we know things of great worth are costly—discipleship for example.* "Suppose one of you wants to build a tower. Will he not first sit down and estimate the cost to see if he has enough money to complete it? For if he lays the foundation and is not able to finish it, everyone who sees it will ridicule him, saying, 'This fellow began to build and was not able to finish.' Or suppose a king is about to go to war against another king. Will he not first sit down and consider whether he is able with ten thousand men to oppose the one coming against him with twenty thousand? If he is not able, he will send a delegation while the other is still a long way off and will ask for terms of peace. In the same way, any of you who does not give up everything he has cannot be my

---

[3]1 Corinthians 6:20

disciple.''[4] Jesus was not one to mince words, was He? Simple and direct—discipleship costs plenty. In fact, He said, it costs everything. What have you got? It will take it all that and more. It will also take all you ever hope to have. Cost counters know that and, even so, know it's worth every bit of what it costs.

*Cost counting requires that we first count the cost, then pay the price, and finally release it once and for all if we are ever to fully have our heart in it.* Proverbs says it like this, "Do not eat the food of a stingy man, do not crave his delicacies; for he is the kind of man who is always thinking about the cost. 'Eat and drink,' he says to you, but his heart is not with you."[5]

Did you ever know anyone who made a sacrifice for you and then never let you forget it? Have you ever done it yourself?

Have you ever done it to God? Given to missions, pledged handsomely to the church's building program, spent late nights rehearsing the Easter musical—then in a time of need reminded God how much He owes you?

Tough questions, aren't they? Yet, cost counting is an important principle successful crossroads navigators always make decisions by.

Two simple questions pretty well sum it up: What will it cost? Am I willing to pay the price? Kind of narrows the list of options even further, doesn't it? Well, good. That's what it's supposed to do.

Some of the options we considered really looked good at first, but during the evaluation of counting the cost they lost their appeal. They simply didn't stand up to the cost involved. However, a few still remain. They are worth the cost. Worth the risk and investment required. Then, believe it or not, twenty-six chapters into a book about making decisions, we are finally about to do just that—ready? It's decision time.

Let us tell you the story of Mark and Dalene and their wonderful decision.

---

[4]Luke 14:28–33
[5]Proverbs 23:6–7

# 26

# You *Can* Get There From Here

---

### Crossroads Principle #3
**No one else can make your decision or
benefit by your mistakes.**

---

"What shall we do, Pastor?" Mark looked from me (Zane) to his young wife, Dalene.

For four years God had blessed the ministry of Mark and Dalene in our church. The impact they were having on the lives of the youth in our congregation was life-changing. Their musical abilities had led our children into levels of worship not often experienced by those so young. Our solid missions program was established under the passionate leadership of this young couple.

Since early childhood, Mark and Dalene have not only sensed God's call to missions, they know they are to minister in Bangladesh. Those involved in their lives know the call to be pure and the field they are drawn to more difficult than perhaps anywhere in the world.

Looking at the young couple that morning in my office, I became more aware than ever of their strong ministerial gifts and God's call on their lives. I know without a shadow of a doubt that they are destined to be a crucial part of a new missions thrust. I recognize something within them that indicates they will be a significant part of a new generation of missionaries that have the potential to revolutionize the entire missions endeavor and impact the world for Christ.

But now, through their tears, I could see that God was leading them in a new way, a way that would teach them how to walk in an abiding kind of faith and trust. To make a decision that almost seemed like an out-of-the-way, round-about choice that didn't lead them closer to Bangladesh, but perhaps even away from their cherished calling.

I could see their struggle. They loved Jan and me, and we loved them. They loved the church here, and the people loved them. But they had an opportunity to serve as short-term missionaries in Hong Kong—a year as missionaries under a great man who could teach them much about missions, Dalene's father.

Dalene's father needed an associate who was willing to be versatile in ministry. Someone who was willing and able to work in singles ministry, youth, and with couples. Basically, to assist in the enormous task of pastoring an international congregation of several thousand members.

Now they sat before me, seeking not only my permission and blessing but guidance and counsel. They had more at stake here than staying in Oakhurst or going to Hong Kong. What they wanted more than anything was the assurance that their decision was in God's will. A decision I struggled with as well, on more than one occasion.

"What makes this so difficult is that we can see that our work here is not finished. We had hoped to come to more completion before we moved on to new areas of ministry. We don't want to leave before it's time." Mark leaned forward and rubbed his hands together. "Whether we go or whether we stay, we want to be within God's will."

I resisted the urge to gather this young couple within the circle of my arms and assure them that God's will is being done. I wanted so much to tell them that finding the will of

God in making our decisions isn't as hard as we make it.

We make it so difficult. We've somehow been conditioned to believe that if we make a decision and "miss the will of the Lord," we're almost certain to be condemned forever. Once we miss it, make a mistake or a wrong decision, we then live forever outside, or at best on the fringes of His will for our lives. We then believe God relegates us to a second-choice position in His kingdom. Certainly never to be used to our full potential or level of giftedness.

How wrong we are! God is not watching every minute, just waiting for us to make a wrong move, poised to squash us with His giant foot or banish us forever to serve Him from some remote or awful place.

Certainly it's important that we don't move in presumption, asking that He bless our plans while disregarding His guidance and will for our lives. Nor do we advocate living in rebellion, disobeying His revealed will for our lives.

However, I look at *missing* the will of the Lord and *rebelling* from it as two entirely different things. On the one hand, take Jonah. He didn't miss the will of the Lord—he rebelled against it and refused it. Supposed to go north, Jonah went south. Told to go to a specific city, he went as far in the opposite direction as possible.

But that's entirely different than honestly trying to obey the will of the Lord and making a mistake. Think again of Jonah. "Go to Nineveh" was as clear a direction as anyone had ever received from God. If Jonah had simply taken a wrong turn, gotten distracted or lost along the way God could have said, "Hey, guy, what are you doing here? This is not where I intended you to be. Nineveh is over that way."

"Oh, sorry Lord," Jonah could have said. "Thanks, I'll get right over there." Jonah's story would have had a much different plot line, wouldn't you agree? He could have spared himself a lot of pain and the big fish an upset stomach.

You see, God doesn't hate us—He's not mad when we make a mistake. He understands when in our humanness we make a mistake and take even unnecessary detours or round-about ways to get where He is sending us.

I began to share with Mark and Dalene my own experience of coming to pastor in Oakhurst.

My wife, Jan, and I had served for fifteen years under the same man now calling Mark and Dalene to Hong Kong. We were secure and happy being on staff in a large church in Phoenix, Arizona. Part of a church-planting team working alongside Pastor Cloud had been a wonderful and rewarding experience. I was content to remain as associate for the rest of my life. I had no idea life was about to change so quickly.

Pastor Leroy and Janice began to sense God's tug toward missions. "Zane," he said, "you're going to pastor our church now." Everybody who loved us just assumed that we'd step into the senior pastorate's position. Transition would be smooth and life would go on as usual—but they were wrong.

For two years I wrestled. Each month the intensity of the struggle grew worse. Groomed, I thought, for the senior pastorate at this church, Jan and I were unsettled, a stirring began deep within.

*"I have another plan,"* we could almost hear God whisper as He spoke quietly within our hearts. *"I have a plan to do a work within you and I have a plan that will bring about that work."*

Jan and I loved the church we were in. We loved the city of Phoenix and we loved being near our families. We felt settled. But, what once seemed so natural and secure began to feel uncomfortable.

We felt challenged to consider pastoring in another place— a place where the path had not been so clearly cut for us. Who knows? Maybe Pastor Cloud is right, maybe someday we will go back to the church in Phoenix as pastors. But for now, we were being led in quite the opposite direction.

Once we made the decision, even though we didn't as yet know where we would go, I heard the Lord address my struggle. *"My son, just abide in Me."*

God began to show me—not on tablets of stone or a miraculous finger writing on some blank wall—but within my heart as I spent time in His presence. He began to show me that if I walked with a heart of integrity before Him, and kept my heart pure and clean as best I could, and if I would always choose to be open and available to correction or willing to have Him deal with me on any level, if I wouldn't try to fake God out or try to fool myself, I could never miss Him or His will. Even if I went somewhere that wasn't exactly within His plan, I could trust Him to—in His own way—get me back to where I should be. Then, in the process, He assured me, He would teach me great lessons. Even if I made a mistake or a wrong decision, as long as I maintained integrity of heart before Him, it wouldn't be wasted time or energy, but preparation and growth. In other words, He assured me that when I did what I thought was the best thing to do, what I thought to be His will, even though I might make an honest mistake from time to time, as long as I walked in integrity it would be all right—I would be all right.

As I shared with Mark and Dalene that day, it seemed so clear how God had coaxed me through my decision.

Accepting the pastorate in Oakhurst, we were finally making the move. I drove the U-Haul truck and Jan the car pulling a trailer. But I must admit. I was scared. The thought of moving my family to California made me nervous. I didn't want to raise my kids as part of what was called "the California lifestyle"—whatever that is. I was sure that earthquake country was not where I wanted to live! However, here we were, on our way.

Self-pity began to whimper inside my head *I don't know anyone there. I don't have any ministerial contacts. This can't only be 900 miles from home—it must be more like 900,000!*

Down the long flat stretch of the interstate between Indio and Banning the wind blew hard against the side of the truck. Sand swirled and smashed teasingly against the windshield. My stomach suddenly gripped with deep fear, I could no longer hold in my emotions. "My, God," I cried, "what am I doing? I'm taking my family away from the support of their friends and family." I couldn't help it. I began to sob.

"What's the matter, Dad?" Deron asked from his place beside me on the seat. The dog sitting between us looked mournful and Deron wrapped his arms around his pet. "What's wrong?"

I wiped the tears from my eyes on the back of my sleeve. "Nothing, son." I tried to reassure him as well as myself.

*"That's right, son,"* God whispered into my spirit. *"Nothing's wrong. You can't miss me. Don't you know I'm with you always?"*

All I had to do was trust in God—not in my decision. Taking steps of faith, trusting that if I were making a mistake, God would help me correct it. I hadn't heard the clear ring of God's voice, saying, "Go ye to Oakhurst." But I hadn't heard him say stay in Phoenix either, in fact, I felt released from that church. All I had to go on was a tug and what *seemed* right. But just as I wasn't supposed to stay in Phoenix, what if I wasn't supposed to go to Oakhurst? What if I wasn't supposed to be a senior pastor? What if I was supposed to find another associate position? What if I failed? What if. . . .

Looking back, and looking at this young couple seeking the Lord's will in very much the same way as I had ten years before, I could see that part of God's overall will for our lives is that we explore and discover the details of that overall will.

His overall will, the big picture of His will for our lives, is often revealed in prayer and through inner relationship with Him. But His specific will is much different. The details of His will is much like knowing where you are headed, the destination, and then planning the route to take to get there.

Think of going to a travel agent and planning a trip to Tokyo. "Let's see," she says, "I can take you out of San Francisco or Los Angeles. Which do you prefer?" She glances at her computer screen. "I can plan an overnight or even a few days in Hawaii; would you like to do that?"

"I want to go to Tokyo."

"Oh, you will. But you have so many choices between here and there. Why not make the most of it?"

It's much the same process when we set out to explore God's will. Taking steps of faith along the way. Even those steps that include times of discovery when we stop and say, "Oh, oh, I don't think I'm supposed to be here. I see now I'm not supposed to be doing this. Now I see where I'm supposed to be—what I'm supposed to be doing. It's all so clear now."

Unless we abandon our misconception that God's will for our lives will be seen as a message scorched across the sky with the blazing finger of God—"Now, child, go to Hong Kong"—we will miss the lessons learned by taking steps of faith and the strength we develop by making decisions. We wait—don't we?—wanting to see the large supernatural message to be written in such a way that the directive of God is undeniable and unmistakable.

Discovering God's will sometimes happens because God allows us to take missteps, showing us for certain where we're not supposed to be. Even making it perfectly clear by those misstep experiences where we're supposed to be. And, the marvelous thing is, God's not mad! He's teaching us to hear His voice by the very experiences we would term as failures.

It was a deep and precious lesson I learned in that U-Haul truck. If I wasn't supposed to be in Oakhurst, God would show me that. I could trust Him. And if I were to be in Salem, or Toledo, Oakhurst was only where I would make my connection and continue on my trip. No matter what, I would get *there* from *here*.

"Jan," I remember saying, "if the whole thing flops and the little church of 100 shrinks to ten in a year, we will not have failed. Because we have not stepped out in presumption, but in faith. We did what in our hearts *seemed* to be God's will. Through this we can discover and learn. And in the end, we will be that much closer to where the Lord wants us."

"What do you want to do?" I asked Mark and Dalene that day.

"We want the will of the Lord." They looked at each other and nodded in agreement.

"I know, guys. That's what makes you unique. That's what makes it so easy for the Lord. You want to do His will. That's what He wants. That's the goal. Now that's settled, what is God's destination, His will for you?"

"Bangladesh," they said without hesitancy.

"Bangladesh, great! When?"

"Not for some time—a couple of years maybe."

"Oh, and until then?"

They looked at each other. I continued. "By way of Hong Kong? You can get there from Hong Kong, you know."

Their eyes opened wide with surprised understanding.

"I know what you want," I said. "You want to go to Hong Kong. You have an opportunity to have some ministry experience beyond what you have here. Experience that will be more to your benefit later in Bangladesh. Don't worry about letting me down. What do you want to do? The Lord will use you in either place."

## What About You?

Obviously, if God has been saying, "Go to Indianapolis," and you go to San Diego, that's rebellion. But if God says, *"I'll use you either place,"* He's giving you an opportunity to have some experiences along the way you may not get any other way.

You've considered the options, you've counted the cost, now it's time to make a decision. Is there a safeguard? A check list to follow? Here are few things that will help.

1. Has God clearly *mandated* that you're to be in Hong Kong, or Cleveland, or take the job across town? If so, it's settled. If not . . .

2. Sometimes the Lord says, "What do *you* want?"

3. Be assured that you won't miss God's will, as long as He has your whole heart.

4. Decision helps us go through the process of discovering on our own, instead of being dependent on someone else to hear the will and word of God for us.

5. Decision helps us come to a new level of trust where we learn that God trusts us to trust Him.

6. The will of God isn't only a destination, or even a decision—it's a heart-settled lifestyle of trust and faith.

7. Decision-making helps us settle issues of obedience—in the heart.

8. Making decisions gives us opportunity to become even more aware of being sons and daughters of God, and trusting Him to show us when we're about to make a mistake or to learn from those we've already made.

9. Even through mistakes, God can teach us deep, precious lessons we could never learn through success.

Does your heart fully belong to God? Is your life completely yielded to Him? Then in faith, knowing God trusts you as much as you trust Him, have the courage and strength to make your decision.

Can we assure you that you're not making a mistake? No, we can't. But we can assure you that even *in* mistakes, you can discover the will of God.

"You know, guys," I said to Mark and Dalene, "God does want to eventually have you in Bangladesh. But that's down the road a ways. What about the meantime? What do *you* want to do?"

"If you wouldn't be hurt, Pastor, we'd like to go to Bangladesh. But we'd like to go to Hong Kong first."

Yes, you can get there from here. And maybe have a stopover in Hawaii on the way! It's your call—it's your decision.

Isn't it time you made it?

# 27

# Walk the Talk

---

**Crossroads Principle #4**

**Take baby steps of faith instead of bold
steps of presumption.**

---

"Rats!" Charlie Brown steps away from the plate, striking
out. Reaching the bench he finds a place by Lucy.

"I'll never be a big league player!" he moans. "I just don't
have it! All my life I've dreamed of playing in the big leagues.
But I know I'll never make it . . . ."

"You're thinking too far ahead, Charlie Brown," Lucy comments. "What you need to do is set yourself more immediate
goals."

"Immediate goals?"

"Yes," says Lucy. "Start with the next inning, when you go
out to pitch. See if you can walk to the mound without falling
down!"[1]

---

[1]"Peanuts" comic strip, July 2, 1972, from the book *Peanuts Jubilee* © 1975
United Features Syndicate.

We laugh at our comic-strip friends Charlie Brown and Lucy—not only because they're funny, but because we identify with them. We all want to make it to the major leagues. Christians are no exception. We read chapters like Hebrews 11 and say, *Wow! I want that kind of big-league faith. I want to be a big league kind of believer.*

But, have we made it to the mound without falling down? There's a truth here we often overlook and, in fact, even avoid:

*Faith that's played out in the milestone moments comes from extensive practice.*

Instead of Charlie Brown, in the Bible we read about David "stepping up to the plate" to face Goliath.[2] "I want to be a giant-slayer, too," we tell ourselves. Or we think about Noah. "I could do that! I could make a boat in the middle of the desert." Then, of course, there's Elisha.[3] Facing the host of Aram, he saw the Lord's host was greater than the king's army. "I know God will protect me—give me a king's army to face!"

We flex our spiritual muscles, stand up tall, and come up to bat as confident as Babe Ruth or Hank Aaron.

But wait a minute! David didn't just step up to fight Goliath. He fought a bear first. Noah and Elisha didn't just stumble into their finest hours of faith—they were prepared for it.

The spotlight of God's Word didn't shine on them because of who they were, but because of what they had come through. Their faith didn't suddenly well up for all the world to see, it was built up when no one was looking.

It wasn't that David, Elisha, and Noah had faith as substance or proof of what God *was about to do* but of the unseen things He had *already done.* David, Elisha, and Noah didn't make it to the big leagues and into the Faith Hall of Fame— Hebrews 11—without making it time and time again "to the mound" without tripping!

No one's life illustrates this fact more than Abraham.[4] We often read about his shining moments. Moments we would call milestone moments. Facing crossroads in which he moved full of faith and grace. Let us not forget that his faith-filled life was not based on a momentary center stage experience, but in walking day by day, responsive to God. Believing

---

[2] 1 Sam. 17:24–36
[3] 2 Kings 6:16
[4] Romans 4

God. Trusting God. No doubt, no wavering, no vague hoping or wishing here. Abraham learned to "walk to the mound without tripping," day after day, month after month, year after year.

And we can too! In fact, it's the first baby step of faith—walking in responsive obedience to God, day by day.

*Faith is learning to live daily in responsive obedience to God.*

The issues of New Testament faith center around discipleship. It is the day-to-day living out of our trust in God, our firm belief in His care and protection. It is the unwavering fixing of oneself, settling one's full weight upon our Father God. It is our absolute commitment to and certainty of God and His Word working within our hearts and making a difference in our lifestyle. And, it is the response of those living with and around us to the unseen (but evidenced in us) that gives our lost and hurting world hope.

In other words, our living confidently and securely in faithfulness gives substantive hope for the hopeless, it provides evidence of the unseen to those who so desperately need to see.[5]

*Faith happens as we walk, not just talk, our faith.*

Faith is not just having confidence and being certain, it launches action. It comes out through our walk, not just our talk. In the twentieth-century westernized Christian culture, we have come to differentiate between "being faithful" and "believing." But scholars tell us that there is very little if any differentiation between them in the language and culture of the Bible. Lifestyle (faithful) and confidence (believing) are so close to being the same it's impossible to separate them.

Mark and Dalene, our young missionary couple now in Hong Kong, illustrate this perfectly. Faithful, dedicated, and committed they worked day after day for four years as if they would be in Oakhurst forever. Their ministry here could never have been mistaken as a stopover or stepping-stone to somewhere else.

I (Zane) have visited them in Hong Kong and seen the same evidence of faithfulness in their work there. Short-term as-

---

[5]Hebrews 11:1, KJV

signment, but long-term effort. Even though they are there only temporarily, they give 100 percent of their hearts and energies to the people of the church and to the leadership under whom they serve.

Mark and Dalene are learning to "walk to the mound without tripping." They are very close to making it into the big leagues—full-time, long-term missionary service.

Are you bored with doing the little things? Is remaining faithful, steadfast, and constant an awful chore? When you are being refined and tested through trial, do you mistake it as warfare and adversarial opposition? Do you get tired of only getting to take a stand, when you'd like to slay a giant? Are you straining against being rooted and grounded, wanting to fly and soar? Is diligence drudgery?

How about prayer? Are you wanting to pray for people and see miracles, but not willing to spend time praying in secret?

What we are really asking you to look at is this: Are you trying to make it into the major leagues without learning to walk to the mound without tripping? In other words, is your faith more *talk* than *walk*?

A decision oftentimes requires little baby steps of faith before the big bold ones. Standing in belief, holding dreams and desires firm within the heart, and praying in secret are the small steps of faith that prepare us for the bold big steps into uncharted horizons. A faithful lifestyle is the prelude to miracles and mighty deeds, not the result.

Your decision awaits your action. And our challenge to you is this: Before you act on your decision, do a reality check on your lifestyle.

You will be required to take a step in the dark, stepping into the unknown with Someone you can't see. Unless your lifestyle has been one of practiced faithfulness and diligent obedience to God's voice and leading, it will be tempting to back out. Suddenly, when faced with your milestone moment of faith, you may revert—to believe that you'd be better off on a visible path or course with an observable guide. If so, you may once again be under the control of one of the power voices that has influence over your life and future.

*Making choices requires taking chances.*

You have reviewed the options, you have counted the cost. Now, if you have been faithful; if your lifestyle has been one of walking faithfully in obedience to God; if you have stood your ground, even at times suffered for your stand; if you have not thrown away your confidence and are willing to pay the price—it's time!

Take your preferred decision to God in prayer. And take the next baby step of faith—wait. For a miracle? No, for the next step to be revealed and made plain. Remember, stepping out in faith is not the same as falling fearfully off the high-diving tower (Chapter 20), it is taking the next step, confident and prepared.

Remember the story of Peter?[6] He was in a boat with the other disciples and they ran into a storm. Waves threatened to capsize the boat when they suddenly saw Jesus walking toward them on the water.

"Lord," Peter said not so confidently . . . "if it's you, tell me to come to you on the water."

"Come," Jesus said.

And what did Peter do? Jump? Hardly. Here was a man who felt fear pumping adrenalin wildly through his whole body. His heart pounding loudly within his chest while tempestuous waves slapped angrily against the boat. His milestone faith moment was not prefaced with "Since you are Jesus, I'm coming out to you!" No, it was "Lord, if it's you. . . ."

The Bible says he came down out of the boat. Picture that. Getting out of the boat meant first he took hold of the side of the boat—the only thing that separated him from the dark water below. Then, did he leap out of the boat as an athlete jumping hurdles? Or, did he put one leg over, then the other while sitting on the side of the boat? Wouldn't you think he put his feet on the water, making sure it would hold him, before letting go of the boat? How long did it take before he stepped one, then two steps away from the boat? What if that had been you?

Peter had walked intimately with Jesus for months, and saw firsthand the miracles. Only months before he had experienced the power Jesus had over the elements, even to calming a sea of turbulence. Yet Peter took small steps of faith toward the Lord he loved so much. Oh yes, he eventually began to sink—but at least he got out of the boat!

Isn't it time you did the same? Come on now, grasp the side

---

[6]Matthew 14:22–32

of the boat. Steady now, that's it, one leg over—now the other!
You can do it!

*Faith is more than just getting out of the boat and walking on the water.*

A commercial aircraft makes its way toward the runway. Its passengers are comfortably settled and they are anticipating their destination. The flight attendants scurry with last-minute duties before strapping themselves in upon instruction of the pilot. Reaching the runway, the pilot pulls the large craft into position, ready and waiting.

This is a picture of where we have come through the processes outlined in this book. The last check by the ground crew has been done and we've been sent out to the runway. This is the fourth baby step of faith.

Like the airline pilot, we wait—for clearance and instructions. The next and most dangerous step of faith is still ahead, take-off. Engines at full speed, you can feel the strain and shudder as the pilot holds the gigantic craft back. Finally released, the enormous engines thrust the lumbering craft down the runway, a series of flap adjustments in the wings respond to the captain's control. Then the laws of gravity work together with the laws of aerodynamics and the airplane soars powerfully toward its cruising altitude.

Reaching the desired elevation, the captain doesn't put the thing on autopilot but expertly oversees all the crew members as together they follow a pre-set course for a distant city. They can't see the city, but they know it's there—all they have to do is stay on course.

Prepared for unexpected rough weather or turbulence, the passengers are told to stay securely belted in their seats. Major storms are avoided when possible, but sometimes the captain guides the passenger-filled craft directly through them. Connected by radio only, he sometimes flies the plane into situations where he cannot see beyond his own reflection in the cabin window.

And the passengers? Do they leave their seats and give the captain suggestions or advice? Of course not, some of them even sleep through the entire flight. They've done their part long before the plane left the gate. They made their plans and reservations. They cleared their calendars and bought their tickets. They packed their suitcases and arranged for transportation at the destination. (What we might equate to baby steps of faith taken long before boarding.) But for now, during the flight, they rely solely on the skill and experience of the captain.

It would be best for us to remember, on the flight of faith, we're the passengers, not the Captain. It's best to leave the pilot-type responsibilities to the expert, wouldn't you agree?

Oh yes. Please, keep your seat belt securely fastened. You just never know—you might need it.

# 28

# Buckled Up for Safety

---

## Crossroads Principle #5
### Stay within God's boundaries.

---

No matter what, Rhonda would not stay in the playpen. She strained against the side and whined and whimpered to get out. She reached toward her mother, father, or anyone who came near. The toys inside were not the right toys, nothing pleased her. Her younger sister Sandy, on the other hand, played contentedly within the boundaries of the playpen.

As a mother, I (Neva) learned an important lesson from watching my young daughters.

Rhonda had not been introduced to a playpen until her baby sister came. Used to having the run of the house, climbing chairs and rummaging through kitchen drawers, she didn't like the sudden change and restriction. Sandy, on the other hand, began her life in our household with a few minutes spent in the playpen every day. As she stayed awake longer, she spent more time there. Sitting squarely in the middle, she contented herself with her toys. She even showed signs of discomfort when allowed out for extended periods of time. She tentatively explored the living room, and crawled down the hall a time or two. But more frequently she stood at the playpen wanting to get back in.

More than once I looked at my babies and wondered if I wasn't like the older one when it came to living within God's boundaries. Used to having free expression of my will, playing and involving myself with whatever I saw or whatever fascinated me, I explored territory that was even dangerous at times.

God would remind me of His Word and the boundaries and standards He set for my life, and I screamed in protest. I wanted to be free of restriction!

Recently, on a newscast, a curfew was established in a city in an effort to cut down on teen crime. "For your own protection," the police told a fourteen-year-old picked up in an abandoned house with several other young teens.

"I don't need protection," the youngster said. "I want to have the full teenage experience."

Her mother was interviewed by the news team. "I'm furious," she said. "My daughter told me she was going to be at a friend's house. That's not the same as going with a friend to an abandoned one!"

Drive-by shootings, hit and run accidents, illegal drugs, and teen pregnancies all speak of a society without limits or boundaries. Too many Christians have the same mind-set as the two-year-old resisting the playpen and the fourteen-year-old complaining about too many restrictions. But we're adults; we understand the wisdom of restricted speed on the freeway, traffic signals, shoplifting laws, and personal freedoms responsibly lived out within boundaries. Don't we?

Remember when the seat belt law was passed? How many protests did we hear or even express about our freedom being snatched away? Seat belts save lives, maybe even yours—giving you the freedom to live a long, healthy, and productive life.

And who can explain the negative attitude toward wearing motorcycle helmets? The mother who lives with her adult son who struggles to cope with daily life because of a head injury sustained in a motorcycle accident can't. An emergency room doctor who has seen brain matter brought in a zip-lock bag alongside a dead patient certainly can't explain why anyone would object to wearing a helmet.

Freedom without restriction isn't freedom—it's dangerous.

Facing crossroads decisions, one must be belted in. Cross-roads are dangerous intersections. If we don't stay within God's boundaries, we could get wounded or even killed! Restrictions that God sets are for our good, and even provide ultimately for freedom within boundaries.

Legalists make living within boundaries a fine art. So exact and difficult, legalism is too hard to follow consistently and still have room to breathe. Legalism isn't what we're talking about here. Legalism isn't living within boundaries—it's prison. You see, God isn't interested in penning you up—but in setting you free. But His goal is liberty, not license. Not freedom to do what you want, but freedom to do what He asks.

Liberty isn't the absence of boundaries, but the skill of living freely within them. It's contenting ourselves with what He gives us, not straining against His boundaries to have unrestricted access to practices, attitudes, and habits that harm us.

Living within God's boundaries isn't too hard. It simply means we accept His Word as the pattern for our lifestyle. Living His lifestyle under His lordship. But, do we believe it? Do we practice it?

Some Christians are like the lady who wouldn't wear her seat belt because it wrinkled her dress. But after the accident, her dress was too bloody to bury her in. Or the baby who cried so loudly that his mother let him out of his car seat, and then a highway patrol officer had to pull the baby's body off the gear shift that had pierced his little chest.

Remember the report of the airplane coming in for a routine landing and hitting an unexpected air pocket and plummeting several hundred feet, slamming several unbelted passengers against the ceiling? Was the uncomfortable seat belt more or less comfortable than being tossed around in the cabin of the aircraft?

How many Christians do you and I know who claim they have been singled out for enemy attack but who are really "unbelted" believers? How many times have we stayed awake all night, wondering how we're going to stretch and make it through the next day because we refuse to live within God's boundaries? And how many times have we received advice to have faith for God's deliverance and support when we really knew deep within we needed to repent and fall upon His mercy instead?

You have come so far. This book has been an inward journey. You've dealt with prayer, learning to listen to God's voice and your identity in Christ. You've learned about God's involvement in your daily life and chosen to unload excess baggage. You've decided to put the past in the past and rebuild the broken foundations of your life. You've learned the value of being open to change and decided to become responsible. You've responded to the challenge of becoming a Champion world-class Christian and make the commitment to the vision God has for your life.

You've purposed to discover and explore God's will. To become a doer of God's Word. You've learned to manage your own spiritual health and maintain your own faith. You've come to know the value of healthy interdependence with other Christians and face life's challenges with integrity. You've purposed to face life as a perseverer, to become an overcomer and not just live life hanging on—but moving on.

And right here, even after all you've learned, you could blow it! If you don't also principle your life and make it your personal policy that from here on in you'll live within God's boundaries, you are at unnecessary risk.

Choosing His boundaries doesn't mean you will become a legalistic tyrant or bore, but that you'll keep your heart undivided and whole in love for Him and Him alone as your one and only God. That you'll keep yourself pure and honest in relationships, keeping your body for your marriage partner only. That you'll guard yourself against bitterness, anger, hatred, and envy.

Living within God's boundaries means living life at God's best level. It means that you'll be able to choose to see every crossroads within view of the larger picture God has for your life—your mission, your message, your future.

Think of the options you are considering right now. Can you live them out—could you choose them and stay within God's boundaries? Do they represent God's best?

Successful crossroads navigators are really just seat-belted Christians. They get to go wherever other Christians go. Traveling to many distant places, having a multitude of varying experiences, but the difference is this—they do it with reduced risk. Buckled (and helmeted) up for safety! It's not freedom-infringing—it's a principle.

# 29

# Being a Seasoned Christian

---

### Crossroads Principle #6
**Stay open to learning even more of
God's will.**

---

"There is a time for everything, and a season for every activity under heaven: a time to be born and a time to die, a time
to plant and a time to uproot, a time to kill and a time to heal,
a time to tear down and a time to build, a time to weep and a
time to laugh, a time to mourn and a time to dance, a time to
scatter stones and a time to gather them, a time to embrace and
a time to refrain, a time to search and a time to give up, a time
to keep and a time to throw away, a time to tear and a time to
mend, a time to be silent and a time to speak, a time to love
and a time to hate, a time for war and a time for peace."[1]

Seasoned Christians know that while God's boundaries

---

[1]Ecclesiastes 3:1–8

and laws remain constant, seasons change. It is only as we are open to the changing seasons of our lives that we remain flexible and open to God's direction and sense His guiding hand on our lives.

For example, I (Zane) have told you about the seasonal change when I moved from being an associate to becoming a senior pastor.

And, I (Neva) have seen my children grow up and leave home, establishing homes and families of their own while ushering in the empty-nest season for me.

We have both experienced seasonal changes—and we both know we will experience even more. And so will you.

The winds of change are even now stirring as you read and consider the concepts we have presented in this book. As you carefully consider each of your options, count the cost, and take baby steps of faith, the seasons of your life are changing. As you learn new things, step out into new spiritual territory, you can see the leaves of your life change color, preparing for an entirely new season of growth.

Even after we have made decisions, taken a step of faith, and planned our approach, we don't have to look at God's will as something we knew once and then continued on in our own strength and wisdom. We can experience the constant awareness of God's will, know fine-tuning course corrections, and avoid unnecessary turbulence, if we principle our lives with staying open to His will as a constant reference to our decision-making processes.

### Don't get ahead—don't fall behind.

One way to stay open to God's will is to stay as close to the center of it as possible. Running ahead of God, simply because He has shown you what lies before you, or lagging behind because you fear or dread what He has shown you, keeps you from experiencing the quietness of the calm center.

### Don't try to force—do try and test.

Never be afraid to question God. That is not to say doubt God and attempt to hold Him accountable. But asking, checking out, keeping communication open is neither intimidating nor irritating to our Father God.

Is this the way, Father? Is this the plan you have for me? Is the ministry you have for me over there? Is that the one you want me to share Christ with? How do you want this done, God? Is this the best way to do this? How do you want me to handle this, Lord?

*Don't start, continue, or end in the flesh that which was begun in faith.*[2]

Nothing is more pathetic than a Christian trying to manipulate God and trying to make it sound like a "new revelation" or "confession of faith." God's Word isn't to be picked apart verse by verse and used like trump cards to gain advantage. It's for correction, reproof, and sound doctrine. We don't change life and circumstances by coating it with Bible passages, we let Bible passages seep deep within our spirits and change us and how we handle circumstances. We let God's Word penetrate us, influence our decisions, and give us His perspective—then *we* manage even difficult circumstances differently because we are changed!

*Let God's will happen.*

Doing His love. Doing His grace. Doing faith. Doing His work. Doing His Word. Then, God's will happens within our hearts, before it happens in our circumstances. Before we possess the promises, His promises must possess us! Living with His promise burning brightly within our hearts, we learn to move within His will, in His way, in His time.

*Don't dictate specifics—ask for them.*

Many approach life as if they are standing in a long hotel hallway lined with closed doors. They expect God to open one from the inside, stick His head out into the hallway and beckon them to come on in. And, perhaps that's the way it is, in the beginning.

But later, others have learned that God goes before them down the hallway, securing the doors He doesn't want opened and unlocking the ones He does. Then in trust and love, the Christian begins the walk of faith, trying each door, turning away from those that are locked and tentatively opening only those that are unlocked.

Seasoned Christians don't hammer away at locked doors,

---

[2]Galatians 3:3. "Are you so foolish? After beginning with the Spirit, are you now trying to attain your goal by human effort?"

shouting and demanding to know what's behind it—they patiently continue down the hallway, testing other knobs.

Seasoned Christians don't even go in the first open door, they simply note which are unlocked and proceed to find all the other unlocked ones (considering options). Once they have discovered what's behind each unlocked door, they pause in the hallway to find out if God has a preferred door. If not, they faithfully indicate their choice and wait for His assenting nod.

*Put decisions in God's hands—and leave them there.*

There's no reason to be obsessed with the need to find answers. Energy would be better invested in seeking God than wasted by pursuing answers. God knows when you need more information and when you can handle more insight. The secret is in the seeking, staying open to God's Word, His touch upon our hearts, and patiently trusting Him for guidance, at just the right time.

*Seasoned Christians are led, not driven.*

Pressures, impatience, circumstances, and emotional needs are cruel and unrelentless drivers. Circumstances can drive you to find resolution, or they can lead you to Christ to find peace. Inner compasses can drive you to your own selfish end, or they can point you to a Savior who knows your needs more than you do. Desires and appetites can drive you into a compulsive-behavior-oriented lifestyle or show you a real hunger and thirst that cannot be satisfied outside of Christ's love and care.

*Seasoned Christians know they cannot always stay within their comfort zones.*

Stretching, reaching, and learning is how we grow. The little girl played appropriately in the playpen until she was old enough to move freely within the boundaries of the backyard. Eventually, though, she was old enough to even ride her bike to the end of the block and back.

Driver's training only lasts until the driver's license is issued. Scary? Of course, and not only for the new driver, but for the protective parent as well.

Seasoned Christians are growing Christians. They look at each experience as a learning one. They don't insist on riding with training wheels once they have learned to keep their balance. Once their lives have track records of faithfulness, seasoned Christians leave their comfort zones and take those bolder steps of faith.

*Seasoned Christians know when it's time to take a risk.*

Recklessness? No, certainly not. But being a Christian is risky business at times. We lay it all on the line, we submit to the decisions and desires of others occasionally. We give up the security of belonging to the world as much as Peter did when he left the solid bottom of the boat behind for a tentative walk on the unsure surface of the water.

When we identify with Christ, we abandon our identity with the world. When we step out in faith, we sometimes risk our reputation and maybe even the respect or understanding of others.

*Seasoned Christians know when it's time to review.*

It takes courage to say, "I need to try something else, this isn't working." Or, "I thought this was God's will, but I see now I made a mistake."

Seasoned Christians know when to scrap a plan or program that worked in 1972 but doesn't in 1995. Seasoned Christians know that what God permitted when we were new in the faith, He might not tolerate after we've walked with Him for twenty years.

*Seasoned Christians expect change.*

Seasoned Christians hold possessions lightly and only a few relationships tightly, knowing that sometimes seasonal changes means everything changes. They live, referring to Ecclesiastes 3, as a farmer does the annual almanac. They look for the best time to plant, watch for the right time to uproot; they sense when to hold close and they don't hold on when the season comes to let go.

Seasoned Christians look at crossroads experiences as indicators that the seasons are once again changing. In fact, it's an underlying principle. It is the principle that tells them, much like the traffic signal, when to wait and when to walk.

Life's most dangerous intersections are almost entirely safe when you go with the signal!

# 30

# New Time, New Place, New Beginnings

---

### Crossroads Principle #7
**Give every choice an honest chance.
Transition is part of reaching every goal
and the immediate result of
every decision.**

---

Transition is a normal part of life. Just knowing that *should* make it easier, but it doesn't always. The toddler, learning to balance and adjust to life from a vertical perspective, will often give up and crawl when he's in a hurry or discouraged by falling down repeatedly. Parents are forced to make the transitions of growth and learning along with their children.

We all experience times of transition. and we all experience a transition following a decision. We make vocational transitions out of and into new jobs. We make transitions from being engaged to being married and then to being parents.

Each relationship we cherish grows and changes. We go through financial transitions. Stretching the budget, experiencing the lay-off, and "faithing" our way through difficult days.

In Christ, and in our relationship with Him, transition serves a purpose. It helps us grow and stretch. It is the way God brings us into new times and new places, to live at new levels of relationship with Him and the unfolding of His will for and in our lives.

Just when life gets comfortable, when it seems to be going smooth and we begin to think we have it all "wired"—we are faced with a decision and ultimately with transition. However, sometimes we discover what we thought was comfort was really a sort of stiffening. We weren't perfecting our faith, we were petrifying in our comfort zone! Transition is what helps us loosen our stiff, spiritual joints and stretch out those belief muscles. And it's not easy.

Do you remember the big rock-climbers we described in Chapter 21? One climber said that almost 80 percent of five-day climbs are canceled by the second day out. Until they make the shift in orientation to having their solid base *in front* of them instead of *beneath* them, climbers try to find almost any excuse to come back down to level ground.

How many can recall trying to ignore or deny the very real effects of traveling to another time zone? Jet lag may seem like a silly complaint to some, but to others it is a real transitional dynamic to be reckoned with.

It is the same when we make decisions. God has indicated that there is to be a change. Only the foolhardy will enter a change without anticipating and planning a strategy for success during the inevitable time of transition. Our friends, the mountain climbers, have a very detailed strategy to make it through their shift of reorientation. They work through intense organizational decisions, carefully organize responsibilities, and express clear expectations—on the ground, before the climb begins. To successfully go through our transitions, we would do well to do likewise.

A good strategy for transition would include the following:
*Understand and expect transition.* This will probably be the most uncomfortable and difficult time of putting your decision into place, but transition is temporary. Give yourself permission to be awkward and disoriented for a time. Being

neither *here* nor *there*. Being *here* but feeling like you're still back *there*—or sensing that though you are *here* you'd rather be over *there*: These are all common complaints of being in transition. Frustration of being neither here nor there is normal and it will pass, given time.

*Be strong.* This is the beginning of a new time, a new place—even a new thing. If you have carefully considered each option, counted the cost, and stepped out in a carefully prepared step of faith, it means that now you must remain strong. Not strong-willed, nor with strong demands, but simply remaining strongly steady.

Never is it more important to maintain the discipline of good devotional habits than in times of transition. How easy to get busy and sidetracked, even with good things, when our schedules and daily routines have been upset by transition. Have your devotional material carefully chosen and readily available to provide encouragement during an anticipated time of transition.

*Be faithful.* A friend recently took a new position and has several months to remain at her present one. I (Neva) had a brief conversation with her one afternoon. "I can't seem to keep my mind on what I'm supposed to do here," she said. "I want so badly to be up there in my new office at my new job. It's terrible!"

My advice? Stay faithful. Character is tested in transition. Leaving loose ends, making it more difficult for the person stepping into her old position, is not the mark of a faithful person. Seeking ways to make the transition easier for the one moving into her present job is one way to be faithful.

Others have felt the Lord moving them to a different location or city. Doug is experiencing that right now. A new job, a new city. How awkward, how challenging. This transition is being made even more difficult and complicated by a delay. Doug admits his faithfulness is being tested as he has to find short-term jobs to support his family in the meantime—while he waits for the new job to begin. We could say it like this: When encountering delay—continue to obey.

*Be patient.* Transition takes time. Walk, don't run—remember we have made a commitment to remain open to God's will. Transition cannot be hurried. The work it does within cannot be rushed. Inner changes don't happen overnight. Neither do seasonal ones. Mountain climbers recognize that acclamation takes place well into the climb. It is best to decide to delay any decision to descend until day number three.

Remember, the children of Israel lived in the wilderness of transition until they were ready to possess the land of promise. We too can view transition as a time of preparation—and preparation takes time.

*Stay soft-hearted toward the Lord.* Attitudes can turn sour in transitory time. Often we, like the wilderness-trekking Israelites, are tempted to complain about the skimpy provisions and dusty conditions. After all, why should we live like nomads when the Promised Land is just around the corner? Why stay out here in tents when the destination could be within reach if we tried harder or worked longer?

We don't like sleeping in strange places, we want our own beds! We are tired of having to stay with the group, we want a place of our own! We want to be there, but we murmur about making the transition it will take to get there.

*Trust God.* Take the time of transition to return to a simplicity of love and faith. Don't make huge demands on yourself, but lean entirely on God. Know His power will sustain you and His strong hands can uphold you.

Emotions and inner turmoil can surface, and while they should not be overlooked, they should not be indicators of God's will and direction. Remember the apostle Paul. He began a missionary journey in which everything that could go wrong, did. More than once he longed for home and friends. But he kept going. He knew that circumstances were no indication that God was or was not in the trip. His trust in God was settled before he set out. A settled trust in God settled him.

*Stay connected.* How threatening it can be to come to church or your Bible study group and get the impression that everyone else's life is smooth and steady. It can be so threatening, in fact, we are often tempted to stay home and go it alone. However, it could be a grave mistake to isolate when we are in transition. It's tough to stay connected when the miracle doesn't come, or the announcement to move away has been made. However, this is the very time we need to get closer. Strength, accountability, and encouragement are easier to come by when we're together. "From Him the whole body, joined and held together by every supporting ligament, grows and builds itself up in love, as each part does its work."[1] If you think you don't need other believers during transition, you are only kidding yourself.

You can listen to cassette tapes, read good books (like this one), and watch Christian television, but you need people. People listen, help carry the burden, and share the pain.

*Remember, but don't look back.* Nothing can make transition more miserable than looking back at how easy and comfortable it used to be. Discouragement is often the result of an over-the-shoulder longing look at the past. Remembering where we have been and knowing it was a connection to where we are going, makes transition easier.

We can remember, being grateful for the past and what we've learned there, but also look forward with thanksgiving for what still lies ahead.

*Rest, but don't quit.* Joshua had heard the voice of the Lord.[2] He was to lead the children of Israel into Canaan. Finally, after years and years of wandering, in transition between Egypt and Canaan, they were on the very shores of the river that separated them from their promise. And they rested. Strange, in our way of thinking, that they should rest before the promise, but the Promised Land held challenges of its own. Challenges quite different than those of transition. It is the same with us.

Some mistake resting for quitting. Afraid that if they sit down even one minute, they won't get up again. But we're not talking about quitting, just resting. Your decision awaits its fulfillment, and will require all the strength you can give it. Now, in transition, is the time to rest—not only from what you've come through, but for what you are about to enter.

Take this time of resting to renew your faith in God's direction and reestablish the confidence you will need to press on. Let this rest refresh you as you spend time in God's Word and presence.

"There remains, then, a Sabbath-rest for the people of God; for anyone who enters God's rest also rests from his own work, just as God did from His. Let us, therefore, make every effort to enter that rest, so that no one will fall by . . . disobedience."[3]

Rest, then, is the pause that truly refreshes!

---

[1]Ephesians 4:16
[2]Joshua 1
[3]Hebrews 4:9–11

Has the decision been made? The options considered and the cost fully counted? Then it's time to put faith into action and move forward into the promises of God's will. We can expect His provision, direction, and protection—transition time has come.

Our congregation understands transition very well. Recently we obeyed what we understood to be the will of the Lord—to not only build a new church, but move to a new location. We didn't move far in terms of distance, but made a significant move in what we understood to be our destiny. By faith we sold our 10,000-square-foot building and built a 53,000-square-foot one. Not only that, we built our new facility around the needs of our children, not our adults! Quite risky, and what a challenge.

As we worked side by side (75 percent of our project was built with volunteer labor), we began to see that the unity that developed, and the harmony that grew between us, was part of the process He used to bring us into a new time and a new place for the plans and purposes He has for our church. We couldn't have shared a bigger vision had we not shared this one. We could not have handled the bigger crowd, the bigger expense, and the bigger challenge had we not met and faced the challenges a step at a time as we built together.

As moving day approached, we cleaned out closets that hadn't been cleaned out in years. We got rid of junk stored in hidden places we forgot we had; from every corner, every niche and cranny, we cleaned, organized, and packed. Finally we loaded all the trucks, vans, and pickups we could get and began a caravan down the six-mile stretch of highway to the new church.

*"This is what I want for this church,"* I (Zane) seemed to hear the Lord whisper. *"I have destined this church to be a church on the move."*

I listened.

*"Just as David restored the ark of God to its rightful place, I am placing this body in its rightful place. This represents what I desire for this church. That my glory and my presence be the focal point of your body life—the very center of all you do."*

The ark of God was only a piece of furniture, when you look at it. But it wasn't just any old piece of furniture—the very presence of God accompanied it.

If I had ever doubted, if I had ever been discouraged, I was not at that moment. God's plan was being put into place.

There is no hurrying what God wants to do. He is doing a work within people. God is always about the business of preparing a people—and preparing them to do things His way.

The ark of God dwells today among people who exchange their life for His. His presence lives within and among those who will face each crossroads as a divine intersection and look for Him there.

Will you? Will you face each decision and make each choice, knowing that God is using this time as preparation, and that at each crossroads we are faced with the challenge of growth and the choice to obey? And, will you enter times of transition knowing that God can use it to prepare you for what He has destined for you to become and the ministry He has designed especially for you?

You are a Christian at a crossroads—will you accept the challenges? The choice is yours—yours alone.

# 31

# Christians at Crossroads: The Challenges, the Choices

Remember, we started this book with a simple purpose in mind—helping you, our reader, to see each of the challenges you now face as a crossroads.

We let you in on the secrets that successful crossroads navigators know, we've presented you with the choices they have made. We also explored the fact that successful crossroads navigators have purposed their lives when faced with challenging and difficult decisions. Finally, we gave you solid biblical principles to help you navigate your own crossroads choices.

And, we strongly believe that, just in reading this book, you've made some surprising choices and changes.

When faced with a challenging situation, for example, we hope you once and for all know that God has not forgotten or abandoned you. We also believe that you can look at your circumstances right now and be able to say without a doubt, "God has a plan and a purpose in this."

We know that you can look at even the most trying situation and be able to choose to trust Him enough to show you not only the way out, but the *why* of the challenge you face. It should be fairly obvious by now that we believe you didn't get to where you are by accident—and that you won't move through your challenge by chance.

We hope you have the clear idea that you can decisively, prayerfully seek God—to talk to Him about your situations, and to have Him talk to you about them. For our prayer lives can be based on our resolve to know God, resting in the knowledge that He knows us!

It is clear that we believe you can discover and follow the direction God gives you. You can discern His will for your life and abandon confusion about His purpose and plans for you.

We have intended to challenge you to grow through each choice you face. We know that each decision you make will stretch you and make you to become more of what God intends.

Finally, our prayer is that the Christians reading this book will find help to experience heart-settled, inner, foundational, practical principles to live by. Principles that bring structure when the challenges you face threaten confusion, that show purpose when you can't understand the reasons.

We believe you are on your way to a life that will be lived without compromise—for no other glory than that of our Savior and Lord, Jesus Christ!

Hey, let's live by choice—not chance!